UNDER
ALASKAN SEAS

U N D E R
ALASKAN SEAS

THE SHALLOW WATER
MARINE INVERTEBRATES

BY LOU AND NANCY BARR
PHOTOGRAPHS BY LOU BARR

**ALASKA
NORTHWEST
PUBLISHING
COMPANY**
Anchorage, Alaska

Library of Congress cataloging in publication data:
Barr, Lou, 1938-
   Under Alaskan seas.
   Bibliography: p.
   Includes index.
   1. Marine Invertebrates — Alaska — Identification.
I. Barr, Nancy, 1937-   . II. Title.
QL161.B37 1983   592.09798   83-2549
ISBN 0-88240-235-8

Cover photo and page ix: the shrimp *Lebbeus grandimanus* perches on the anemone *Cribrinopsis fernaldi.*

Design by Cathy Cullinane
Photographs by Lou Barr
Illustrations by Ray Weisgerber

Alaska Northwest Publishing Company
Box 4-EEE, Anchorage, Alaska 99509

Printed in U.S.A.

Contents

Major Marine Water

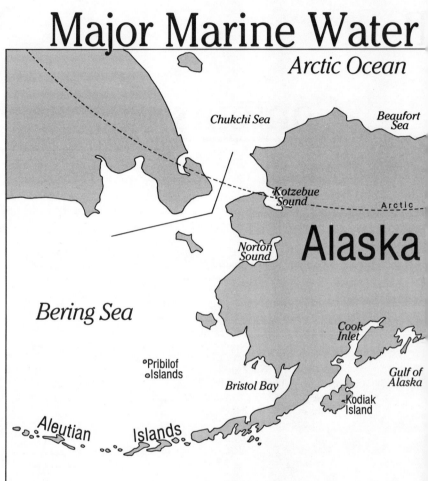

Arctic Ocean

Chukchi Sea

Beaufort Sea

Kotzebue Sound

Arctic

Alaska

Norton Sound

Bering Sea

Cook Inlet

°Pribilof
°Islands

Gulf of Alaska

Bristol Bay

Kodiak Island

Aleutian Islands

Pacific

CartoGraphics by Jon.Hersh

Bodies

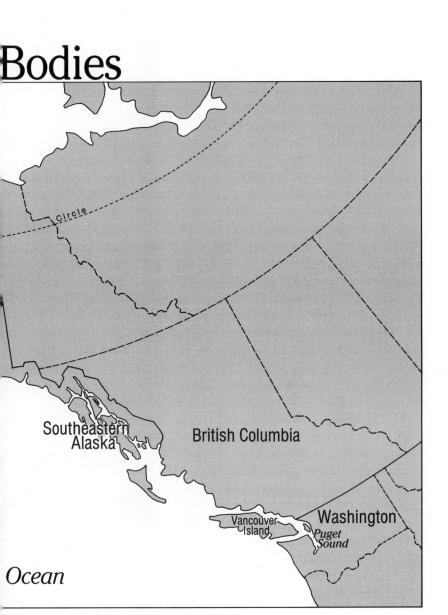

Circle

Southeastern
Alaska

British Columbia

Vancouver
Island

Washington

Puget
Sound

Ocean

Foreword

The coastal waters of Alaska are the source of an almost
endless abundance of living creatures. The invertebrates, or animals without backbones, are one of the
major groups of Alaska's intertidal and shallow water
marine organisms. These animals range from the structurally simple sponges to the more complex anemones,

sea stars, and crabs. Collectively they are a ubiquitous and important part of the life along the coasts. Any Alaskan marine community is likely to include plants, fishes and mammals in addition to invertebrates, but it is the invertebrates that appear most consistently and in the greatest variety and abundance. This book presents a sample of Alaska's shallow marine invertebrates, illustrating them live and in their natural niches, and describing their appearance and their roles in the living systems of which they are so important a part.

Alaska's coastline is both extensive and varied. The general coastal outline of the state measures about 6,000 miles but the total length of Alaska's interface with the sea, a figure that includes all the miles of shoreline wrapped around innumerable straits, headlands, channels, bays and islands, is estimated at close to 47,000 miles —a distance equal to nearly twice the circumference of the earth. This coastline meanders through 20 degrees of latitude from the temperate waters of Southeastern Alaska and the Aleutian Islands to the frigid conditions of the Arctic Coast. In the shallow waters along this enormous stretch of coast is an environment of extreme variety and complexity. The water itself can range from silt-laden and almost fresh near the mouths of the great rivers to clear and highly saline where the oceanic influence dominates. The substrate may be solid bedrock, boulders, gravel, sand or mud. The bottom topography ranges from flat to vertical and may extend into rocky overhangs, deep crevices and caves. Currents that pass over the shallow sea floor may be negligible or swift. Stretches of coast are exposed to the powerful winds and waves of the open ocean while others are protected in bays or in the lee of headlands and islands. Weather and season bring with them modifications of the shores and shallow sea floors, creating an environment of subtle to drastic change from location to location, from season to season, and from year to year.

In an environment which encompasses so many differences and so much change, it is only logical to expect to find a parallel diversity among the kinds and combinations of animals that live there. Invertebrates of many kinds are nearly always present, and they play a large, important part in the communities in which they live. Their forms, feeding habits, means of reproduction, locomotion or protection are almost endlessly varied, and so, too, are their relations to other organisms around them.

Many of Alaska's marine invertebrates are clearly important to us in both positive and negative ways. Crabs, shrimps, and many molluscs are used as high quality food and support valuable commercial fisheries. On the negative side, jellyfish may clog seine or gill nets and irritate the skin of fishermen who handle them. Boring molluscs damage wood in boat hulls and docks. Other invertebrates attach themselves to man-made objects placed in the water, reducing boat speeds through hull fouling and sinking buoy lines by accumulated weight.

The lives of a vast majority of marine invertebrates may seem totally separated from our own, but a close look at the ecological roles of these animals will show that they too are of at least indirect importance to us. Sponges, for example, provide hiding places for some of the shrimps. The young of several marine fishes live among the stinging tentacles of large jellyfish and derive protection from them. Many plankton-eating invertebrates compete for food with young salmon passing through coastal waters. At the same time, other invertebrates or their larvae provide food for salmon, crabs, shrimp and many other animals we seek for our own use. Almost every invertebrate along Alaska's coast contributes in some way to our lives and only our scant knowledge of them keeps us from fully appreciating their impact on us.

The diversity and number of marine invertebrate

species in Alaska is so great that a complete record of them would fill many volumes. Therefore we have chosen to cover only representative animals, basing our selections on two criteria of particular importance. First, we've discussed invertebrates that are common among Alaskan species and most apt to be encountered in exploration of the intertidal and shallow-water marine environment down to about 20 fathoms. As an exception to this, we've included a few organisms just because they are unusual or help represent the total range of animals found within a particular group. Size was the second criterion. Only those invertebrates large enough to be readily observed were included, and in most cases, they can be identified without the use of a microscope.

Many of the invertebrates described here occur not only in Alaska but south along the Pacific Coast to Washington, Oregon, and beyond. Some are also found on the Asiatic side of the north Pacific Ocean or in the north Atlantic Ocean as well. In the text, however, we've given only the animal's geographic range along the west coast of North America.

Geographic ranges, as well as depth ranges and maximum sizes of Alaska's invertebrates, must always be stated provisionally. As the extent of exploration and observation increases, it is almost inevitable that representatives of a species will be found farther, deeper or larger than they were previously known. So it is with some of the species described in this book. We have given maximum ranges and sizes as reported in published literature except in cases where our own observations have extended the reported limits.

All invertebrates described in the text are grouped according to their scientific classification. All living things belong to either the plant or animal kingdom, and within each kingdom, each organism can be further identified by the groups and sub-groups to which it belongs. The Dungeness crab, for example, would be classified as follows:

Kingdom: Animal
Phylum: Arthropoda
Class: Crustacea
Order: Decapoda
Family: Cancridae
Genus: *Cancer*
Species: *magister*

The last two classification levels, genus and species, give an organism its scientific name. Thus, the Dungeness crab is *Cancer magister.*

The text begins with the structurally simple sponges, the phylum Porifera, and proceeds through groups of progressively more complex animals. By turn, the general characteristics of each phylum are given and the major sub-groups defined. Individual species are described under each phylum or its sub-group.

Most of Alaska's marine invertebrates have been scientifically described, and therefore most have a two-part scientific name, which we've included as completely as possible in its current, accepted form. In some cases, however, the name may be preceded by a question mark, an indication that the identification is probably correct but subject to some doubt. Occasionally, only the genus is given, such as for *"Beroe* sp.," because the genus of the invertebrate can be determined with ease, but difficulties arise in pinpointing the species to which it belongs.

Common names pose a special problem in dealing with relatively unknown animals. Few of Alaska's invertebrates have common names because they are not coined until large numbers of people have dealt with the particular species. The common names of those invertebrates that have them are given following the species' scientific name. The common name for the group to which a species belongs is given preceding the first species discussion of the group and/or as a right-hand corner page heading. In no instance have we attempted to coin a new common name for an animal that doesn't already have one.

All efforts have been made to use terms easily understandable to laymen. However, it is not always possible to describe an aspect of appearance or behavior without resorting to technical terms. When such are used, they are explained in the text and glossary or illustrated in drawings.

The photographs were taken underwater with a variety of 35mm photographic equipment, usually using artificial light and slow-speed, fine-grain film for the sharpest possible images.

For identification of particular species and information about them, we are grateful to Richard Haight (hermit crabs), Dennis Lees (hydroids and bryozoans), John MacKinnon (sponges), Dr. Charles O'Clair (barnacles), Dr. Rita O'Clair (annelids) and Dr. Bruce Wing (mysids and amphipods). Dr. Rita O'Clair reviewed the book's section on annelids. Dr. Eugene Kozloff, Dr. Bruce Wing and John MacKinnon reviewed the entire manuscript and generously shared with us their knowledge and their thoughts concerning manuscript format and style.

In general, appreciation is extended to the staff of the National Marine Fisheries Service Laboratory at Auke Bay, Alaska, for their cooperation in affording us access to their facilities during the preparation of this book.

—Lou and Nancy Barr

Photographic Identification

The large number accompanying each species' photograph corresponds to the number found with the species' text discussion. Use the number to quickly move between text and photographs.

1 *Scypha compressa*
Amchitka Island, Aleutian Islands

2 *Scypha ciliata*
Amchitka Island, Aleutian Islands

3
*Geodinella
robusta*
Steamer Bay, Southeastern Alaska

4 *Tetilla* sp.
Amchitka Island, Aleutian Islands

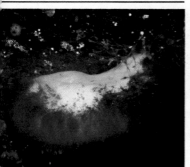

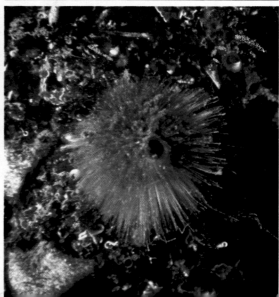

5 *Penares cortius*
Steamer Bay,
Southeastern Alaska

6 *Polymastia* sp.
St. George Island, Pribilof Islands

7
Mycale lingua
Amchitka Island, Aleutian Islands

8
*Myxilla
incrustans*
Steamer Bay, Southeastern Alaska

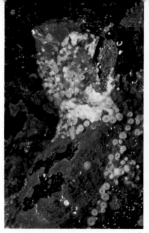

9 *Cliona celata*
Steamer Bay,
Southeastern Alaska

10 *Suberites ficus*
Tenakee Inlet, Southeastern Alaska

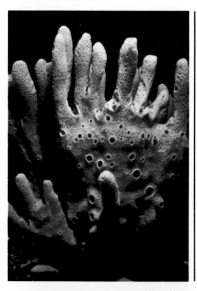

11
Isodictya sp.
Little Port Walter,
Southeastern Alaska

12
Halichondria panicea
Stephens Passage,
Southeastern Alaska

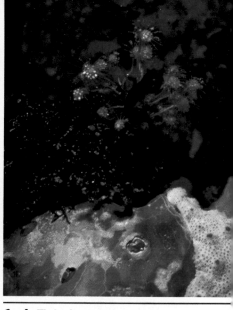

14 *Tubularia* sp.
Otter Island, Pribilof Islands

13 *Corymorpha* sp.
Cape Woolley, Norton Sound

15 ? *Campanularia* sp.
Tenakee Inlet, Southeastern Alaska

16 Family Sertulariidae
Sledge Island, Norton Sound

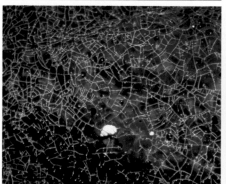

6

17 **? *Aglaophenia* sp.**
Amchitka Island, Aleutian Islands

18 ***Obelia* sp.**
Auke Bay,
Southeastern Alaska

19
Staurophora mertensii
Stephens Passage, Southeastern Alaska

20 **? *Calycopsis nematophora***
Amchitka Island, Aleutian Islands

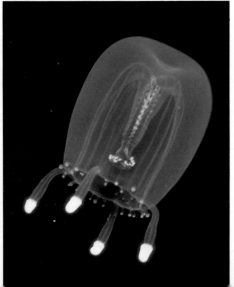

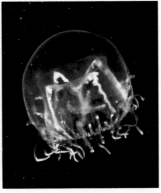

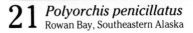

21 *Polyorchis penicillatus*
Rowan Bay, Southeastern Alaska

22 *Eperetmus typus*
Rowan Bay,
Southeastern Alaska

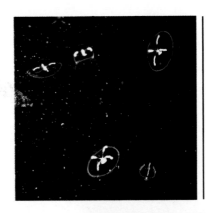

23
? *Eutonina indicans*
Little Port Walter,
Southeastern Alaska

24
Aequorea sp.
Amchitka Island, Aleutian Islands

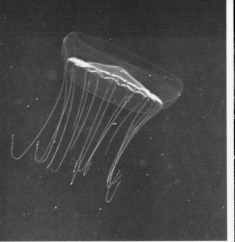

Solmissus sp. **25**
Little Port Walter,
Southeastern Alaska

26 *Allopora campyleca*
Stephens Passage, Southeastern Alaska

Stylantheca porphyra **27**
Little Port Walter, Southeastern Alaska

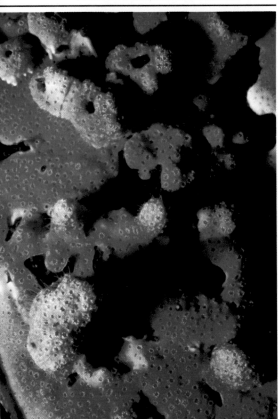

28
Aurelia labiata
Steamer Bay, Southeastern Alaska

Phacellophora
camtschatica **29**
Amchitka Island, Aleutian Islands

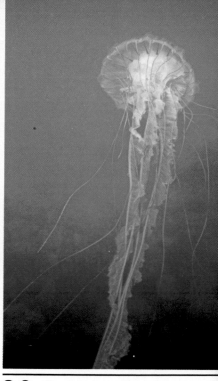

30 *Chrysaora melanaster*
St. George Island, Pribilof Islands

Cyanea capillata **31**
Tenakee Inlet, Southeastern Alaska

32
Haliclystus sp.
Yakobi Island, Southeastern Alaska

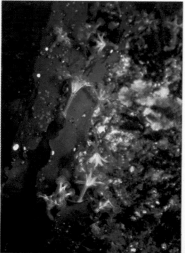

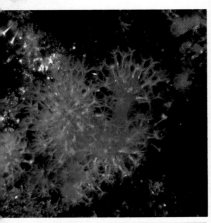

Gersemia rubiformis **33**
Little Port Walter, Southeastern Alaska

34 *Ptilosarcus gurneyi*
Tenakee Inlet, Southeastern Alaska

35
? *Virgularia* sp.
Sea Otter Sound,
Southeastern Alaska

36 Order Gorgonacea
Steamer Rock, Southeastern Alaska

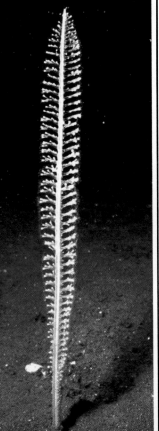

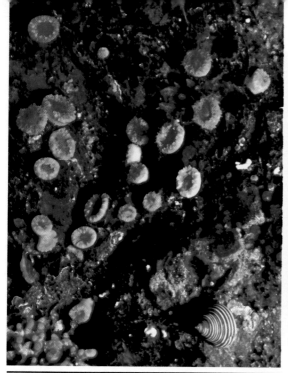

38 *Pachycerianthus fimbriatus*
Kindergarten Cove,
Southeastern Alaska

Balanophyllia elegans **37**
Portlock Harbor, Southeastern Alaska

Epizoanthus scotinus **39**
Schultze Cove, Southeastern Alaska

40 *Metridium senile*
Steamer Bay,
Southeastern Alaska

42 *Tealia lofotensis*
Cape Cross, Southeastern Alaska

Tealia crassicornis **41**
Takanis Bay, Southeastern Alaska

Cribrinopsis fernaldi **43**
Amchitka Island, Aleutian Islands

44 *Epiactis* sp.
St. Paul Island, Pribilof Islands

13

45
*Anthopleura
xanthogrammica*
Etolin Island,
Southeastern Alaska

46
*Anthopleura
artemisia*
Stephens Passage,
Southeastern Alaska

47 *Stomphia coccinea*
Stephens Passage, Southeastern Alaska

14

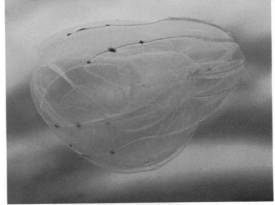

48
Bolinopsis sp.
Amchitka Island,
Aleutian Islands

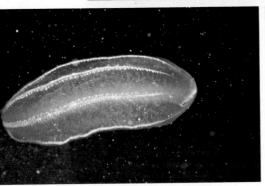

49
Beroe sp.
St. George Island, Pribilof Islands

Pleurobrachia sp. **50**
Steamer Bay, Southeastern Alaska

51 Order Polycladida
Steamer Bay, Southeastern Alaska

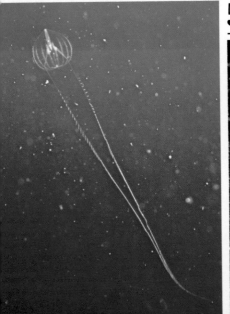

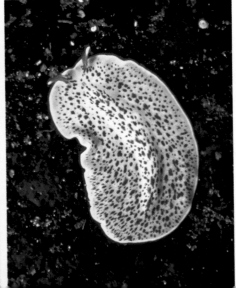

52
*Tubulanus
sexlineatus*
Pybus Bay,
Southeastern Alaska

53
*Tonicella
lineata*
Sitkalidak Island,
Gulf of Alaska

54
*Tonicella
insignis*
Three Saints Bay,
Kodiak Island

55
Mopalia lignosa
Steamer Bay, Southeastern Alaska

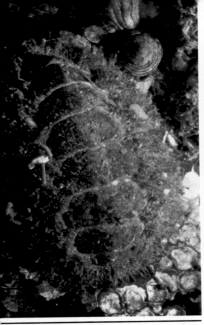

57 *Placiphorella rufa*
Steamer Bay, Southeastern Alaska

Mopalia muscosa **56**
Tee Harbor, Southeastern Alaska

58
*Katharina
tunicata*
Sundstrom Island,
Gulf of Alaska

59
*Cryptochiton
stelleri*
Kruzof Island,
Southeastern Alaska

68 *Calliostoma ligatum*
Steamer Bay, Southeastern Alaska

69
Calliostoma annulatum
Kalinin Bay, Southeastern Alaska

70
Lacuna carinata
Stephens Passage,
Southeastern Alaska

71
Littorina sitkana
Steamer Bay, Southeastern Alaska

20

Littorina scutulata **72**
Steamer Bay, Southeastern Alaska

73 *Epitonium greenlandicum*
Young Bay, Southeastern Alaska

Trichotropis cancellata **74**
Stephens Passage, Southeastern Alaska

75
Natica clausa
McHenry Inlet, Southeastern Alaska

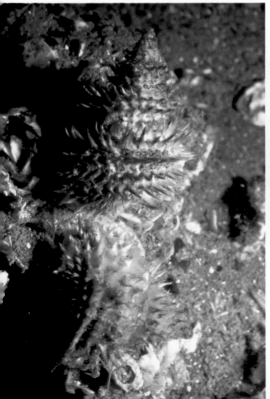

76 *Lunatia lewisii*
Steamer Bay, Southeastern Alaska

77 *Fusitriton oregonensis*
Stephens Passage,
Southeastern Alaska

78 *Nucella lamellosa*
Burnett Inlet, Southeastern Alaska

79 *Ceratostoma foliatum*
Burnett Inlet,
Southeastern Alaska

81 *Amphissa columbiana*
Steamer Bay,
Southeastern Alaska

Boreotrophon stuarti 80
Three Saints Bay, Kodiak Island

82 *Buccinum plectrum*
Stephens Passage, Southeastern Alaska

83
Volutharpa ampullacea
Stephens Passage,
Southeastern Alaska

84 *Colus halli*
Stephens Passage, Southeastern Alaska (NMFS, by Lou Barr)

85 *Neptunea lirata*
Stephens Passage,
Southeastern Alaska

86 *Searlesia dira*
Sea Otter Sound, Southeastern Alaska

87
*Gastropteron
pacificum*
Rowan Bay,
Southeastern Alaska

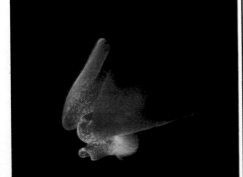

24

88
*Berthella
californica*
Baranof Island,
Southeastern Alaska

89
*Triopha
catalinae*
Stephens Passage,
Southeastern Alaska

90 *Cadlina
luteomarginata*
Stephens Passage,
Southeastern Alaska

91 *Diaulula sandiegensis*
Steamer Bay, Southeastern Alaska

100
Dirona aurantia
Stikine Pass,
Southeastern Alaska

101
*Coryphella
fusca*
Tenakee Inlet,
Southeastern Alaska

103
Aeolidia papillosa
Rowan Bay,
Southeastern Alaska

Hermissenda crassicornis **102**
Rowan Bay, Southeastern Alaska

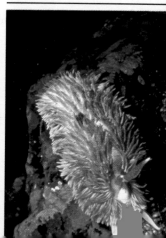

104
Siphonaria thersites
Stephens Passage,
Southeastern Alaska

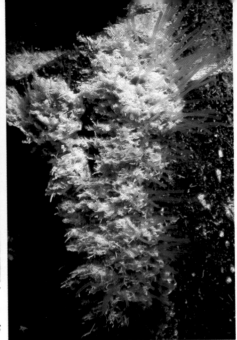

105 *Bankia setacea*
Neets Bay, Southeastern Alaska

107
Musculus niger
Stephens Passage, Southeastern Alaska

106
Mytilus edulis
Pybus Bay, Southeastern Alaska

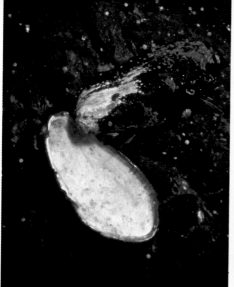

Modiolus modiolus
Steamer Bay, Southeastern Alaska **108**

109
Chlamys rubida
Stephens Passage, Southeastern Alaska

110
Chlamys hastata hericia
Steamer Bay, Southeastern Alaska

111
Pecten caurinus
Stephens Passage,
Southeastern Alaska

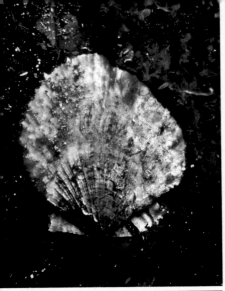

Hinnites
multirugosus 112
Earl Cove, British Columbia

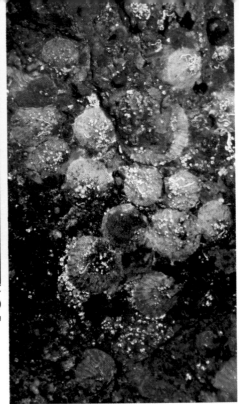

113 *Pododesmus cepio*
Freshwater Bay, Southeastern Alaska

Clinocardium
nuttallii 114
Anita Bay, Southeastern Alaska

115 *Serripes*
groenlandicus
Sea Otter Sound, Southeastern Alaska

117 *Prototheca staminea*
Stephens Passage, Southeastern Alaska
(NMFS, by Lou Barr)

Macoma inquinata
Stephens Passage, Southeastern Alaska **116**

Humilaria kennerleyi **118**
Steamer Bay, Southeastern Alaska

Saxidomus giganteus
119 Stephens Passage,
Southeastern Alaska

32

121 *Hiatella arctica*
Stephens Passage, Southeastern Alaska

Mya truncata **120**
Steamer Bay, Southeastern Alaska

122
Entodesma saxicola
Little Port Walter, Southeastern Alaska

123 *Rossia pacifica*
Steamer Bay, Southeastern Alaska

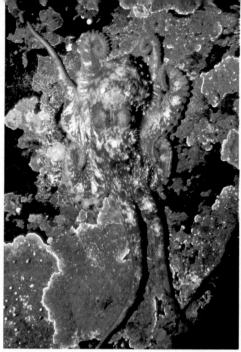

Octopus dofleini **124**
Kalinin Bay, Southeastern Alaska

125 *Nephtys* sp.
Steamer Bay, Southeastern Alaska

127 ? *Harmothoe* sp.
Steamer Rock, Southeastern Alaska

Nereis brandti **126**
Steamer Bay, Southeastern Alaska

128
Trypanosyllis
sp.
Sundstrom Island,
Gulf of Alaska

129
Family Terebellidae
McHenry Inlet, Southeastern Alaska

130 *Pectinaria granulata*
Little Port Walter, Southeastern Alaska

131 *Spiochaetopterus costarum*
Steamer Bay, Southeastern Alaska

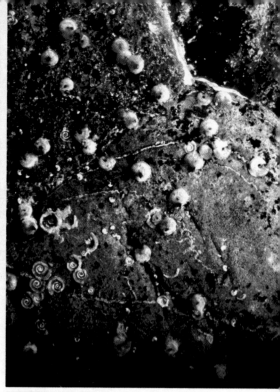

132
Schizobranchia sp.
Little Port Walter,
Southeastern Alaska

133 *Spirorbis* sp.
Stephens Passage, Southeastern Alaska

134 *Crucigera* sp.
Steamer Bay,
Southeastern Alaska

135
Serpula vermicularis
Etolin Island, Southeastern Alaska

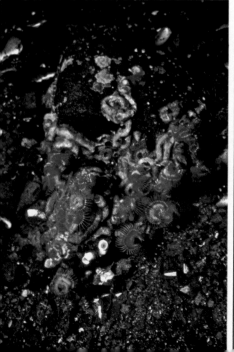

136
Notostomobdella cyclostoma
Stephens Passage,
Southeastern Alaska

Phascolosoma agassizii **137**
Steamer Bay, Southeastern Alaska

138 *Golfingia margaritacea*
Steamer Bay, Southeastern Alaska
(NMFS, by Lou Barr)

139 *Balanus nubilus*
Burnett Inlet, Southeastern Alaska

Balanus cariosus **140**
Stephens Passage,
Southeastern Alaska

141 *Balanus glandula*
Stephens Passage,
Southeastern Alaska
(NMFS, by Lou Barr)

142 *Lepas pacifica*
Steamer Bay, Southeastern Alaska

143 *Neomysis mercedis*
Steamer Bay, Southeastern Alaska

38

144
*Gnorimosphaeroma
oregonensis*
Steamer Bay, Southeastern Alaska

145
Orchestia traskiana
Stephens Passage, Southeastern Alaska

146 *Anonyx* sp.
Little Port Walter, Southeastern Alaska

147 *Pandalus borealis*
Tenakee Inlet, Southeastern Alaska

148 *Pandalus goniurus*
Stephens Passage, Southeastern Alaska

149
Pandalus danae
Little Port Walter, Southeastern Alaska

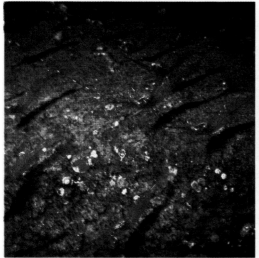

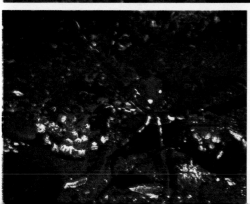

150
Pandalus hypsinotus
Captains Bay, Aleutian Islands

Pandalus platyceros **151**
Little Port Walter, Southeastern Alaska

Lebbeus groenlandicus **152**
Carroll Inlet, Southeastern Alaska

153
Lebbeus grandimanus
Tenakee Inlet, Southeastern Alaska

Crangon sp. **154**
Steamer Bay, Southeastern Alaska

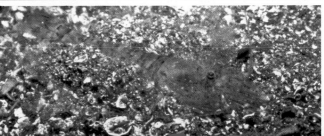

155
Nectocrangon sp.
Hawk Inlet, Southeastern Alaska

156
Hapalogaster sp.
Steamer Bay, Southeastern Alaska

157
Placetron wosnesenskii
Rowan Bay, Southeastern Alaska

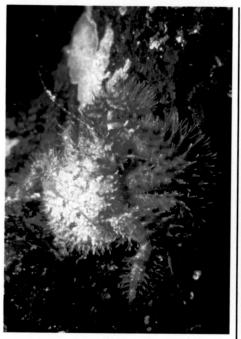

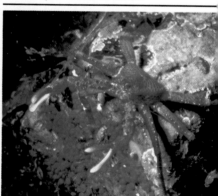

158 *Acantholithodes hispidus*
Hassler Pass, Southeastern Alaska

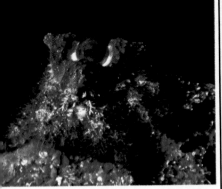

Rhinolithodes
wosnessenskii **159**
Etolin Island, Southeastern Alaska

Phyllolithodes
papillosus **160**
Burnett Inlet, Southeastern Alaska

161 *Cryptolithodes sitchensis*
Kalinin Bay, Southeastern Alaska

162 *Cryptolithodes typicus*
Steamer Bay, Southeastern Alaska

163
Lopholithodes mandtii
Steamer Bay,
Southeastern Alaska

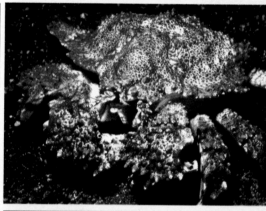

164
Lopholithodes foraminatus
Steamer Bay,
Southeastern Alaska

165
Paralithodes camtschatica
Tenakee Inlet,
Southeastern Alaska

166
Paralithodes platypus
Stephens Passage,
Southeastern Alaska

44

167
Pagurus hirsutiusculus
St. James Bay,
Southeastern Alaska

168 *Pagurus ochotensis*
Stephens Passage, Southeastern Alaska

169 *Elassochirus tenuimanus*
Steamer Bay, Southeastern Alaska

170
Elassochirus cavimanus
Port Frederick,
Southeastern Alaska

171 *Elassochirus gilli*
St. James Bay,
Southeastern Alaska

172 *Discorsopagurus schmitti*
Steamer Bay, Southeastern Alaska

173
Oregonia gracilis
Steamer Bay,
Southeastern Alaska

174
Chorilia longipes
Steamer Bay,
Southeastern Alaska

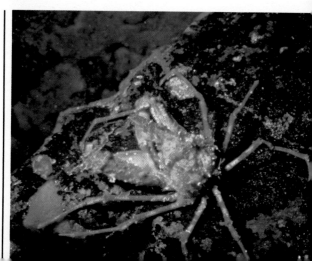

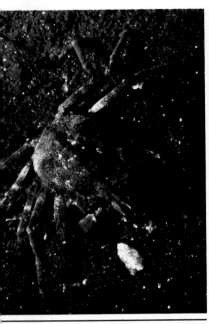

176 *Chionoecetes bairdi*
Funter Bay, Southeastern Alaska

Hyas lyratus **175**
Steamer Bay, Southeastern Alaska

Pugettia gracilis **177**
Tenakee Inlet, Southeastern Alaska

Lophopanopeus bellus **178**
Steamer Bay, Southeastern Alaska

179 *Hemigrapsus nudus*
Steamer Bay, Southeastern Alaska

180 *Telmessus cheiragonus*
Steamer Bay, Southeastern Alaska

181 *Cancer magister*
Tenakee Inlet, Southeastern Alaska

182
Cancer gracilis
Steamer Bay, Southeastern Alaska

48

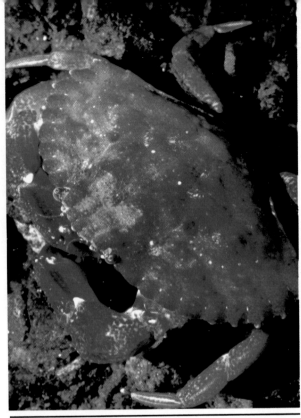

183 *Cancer productus*
Steamer Bay, Southeastern Alaska

184 *Cancer oregonensis*
Steamer Bay, Southeastern Alaska

185
Eucratea loricata
Port Snetisham, Southeastern Alaska

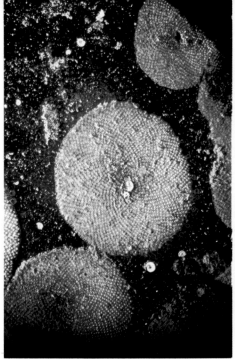

186 *Membranipora* sp.
Stephens Passage, Southeastern Alaska

187 *Carbasea carbasea*
Cape Woolley, Norton Sound

188 *Microporina borealis*
Stephens Passage, Southeastern Alaska

Dendrobeania murrayana 189
Port Snetisham,
Southeastern Alaska

190 **_Phidolopora pacifica_**
Stephens Passage,
Southeastern Alaska

Heteropora sp. 191
Sundstrom Island, Gulf of Alaska

192 **_Flustrella_ sp.**
St. George Island, Pribilof Islands

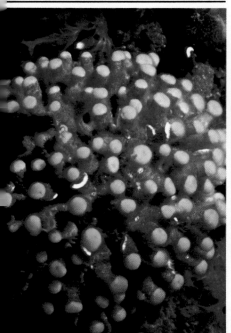

193 *Terebratalia transversa*
Freshwater Bay, Southeastern Alaska

194 *Terebratulina unguicula*
Yankee Cove, Southeastern Alaska

195 *Hemithyris psittacea*
Stephens Passage, Southeastern Alaska

196 Phoronids
Clarence Strait, Southeastern Alaska

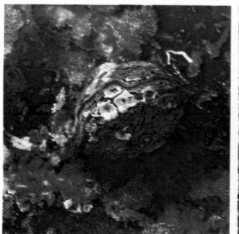

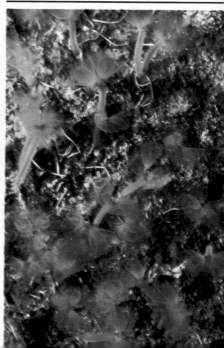

198 *Luidia foliolata*
Anita Bay, Southeastern Alaska

*Florometra
serratissima* **197**
Burnett Inlet, Southeastern Alaska

Mediaster aequalis **199**
Kalinin Bay, Southeastern Alaska

200
Gephyreaster swifti
Tenakee Inlet, Southeastern Alaska

201
Ceramaster patagonicus
Port Snetisham,
Southeastern Alaska

202
Hippasteria sp.
Akun Island,
Aleutian Islands

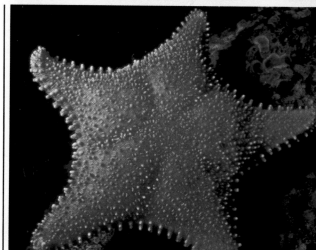

203
Dermasterias imbricata
Steamer Bay,
Southeastern Alaska

54

205 *Solaster stimpsoni*
Sea Otter Sound, Southeastern Alaska

Solaster endeca 204
Rowan Bay, Southeastern Alaska

207
Crossaster papposus
Amchitka Island, Aleutian Islands

206
Solaster dawsoni
Steamer Bay,
Southeastern Alaska

Pteraster tesselatus **208**
Tenakee Inlet,
Southeastern Alaska

209 *Pteraster militaris*
Burnett Inlet, Southeastern Alaska

210 *Henricia leviuscula*
Rowan Bay, Southeastern Alaska

211
Henricia sanguinolenta
Stephens Passage,
Southeastern Alaska

213 *Orthasterias koehleri*
Steamer Bay, Southeastern Alaska

212 *Lethasterias nanimensis*
Stephens Passage,
Southeastern Alaska

214
Leptasterias hexactis
Mouth of Bessie Creek, Southeastern Alaska

215 *Evasterias troschelii*
Steamer Bay, Southeastern Alaska

216 *Pisaster ochraceus*
Steamer Bay, Southeastern Alaska

217 *Pycnopodia helianthoides*
Takanis Harbor, Southeastern Alaska

218
Ophiura sarsii
Steamer Bay,
Southeastern Alaska

58

220
Gorgonocephalus
eucnemis
Little Port Walter, Southeastern Alaska

Ophiopholis
aculeata **219**
Pybus Bay, Southeastern Alaska

Strongylocentrotus
droebachiensis **221**
Tenakee Inlet, Southeastern Alaska

222 *Strongylocentrotus pallidus*
Etolin Island, Southeastern Alaska

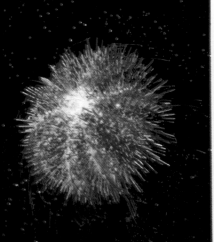

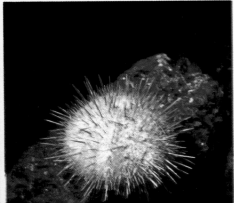

223 *Strongylocentrotus franciscanus*
Clarence Strait, Southeastern Alaska

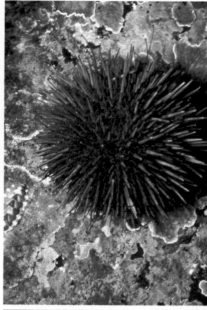

224 *Strongylocentrotus purpuratus*
Takanis Harbor,
Southeastern Alaska

225
Dendraster excentricus
Cape Cross, Southeastern Alaska

226
Cucumaria miniata
Little Port Walter, Southeastern Alaska

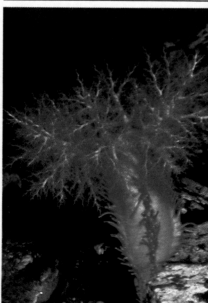

227
Cucumaria vegae
Stephens Passage,
Southeastern Alaska

228
Parastichopus
californicus
Piehle Passage, Southeastern Alaska

229
Eupentacta
quinquesemita
Stephens Passage,
Southeastern Alaska

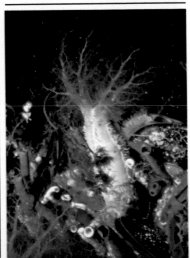

230 ? *Chiridota* sp.
Sea Otter Sound,
Southeastern Alaska

231 *Psolus chitonoides*
Little Port Walter,
Southeastern Alaska

232
Salpa fusiformis
Portlock Harbor,
Southeastern Alaska

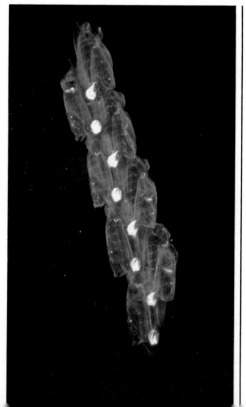

Ascidia paratropa
Little Port Walter,
Southeastern Alaska **233**

234 *Corella willmeriana*
Tenakee Inlet, Southeastern Alaska

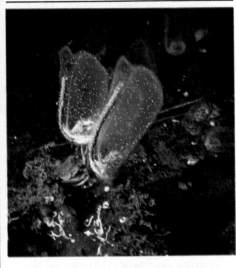

Halocynthia aurantium **235**
Tenakee Inlet, Southeastern Alaska

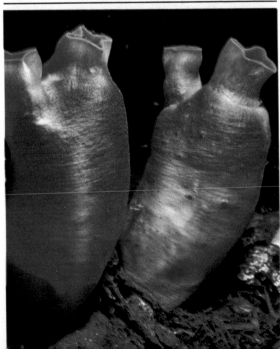

236 *Styela* sp.
Sundstrom Island, Gulf of Alaska

237
Boltenia villosa
Steamer Bay, Southeastern Alaska

238
Cnemidocarpa finmarkiensis
Sea Otter Sound,
Southeastern Alaska

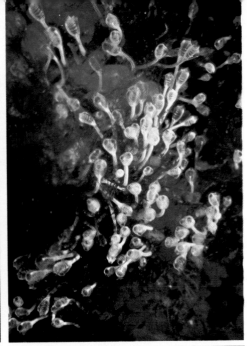

239

Metandrocarpa taylori
McHenry Inlet, Southeastern Alaska

240 ? *Clavelina* sp.
Freshwater Bay, Southeastern Alaska

241 ? *Trididemnum* sp.
Steamer Bay, Southeastern Alaska

Marine Invertebrates

The following discussions of Alaska's marine invertebrates begin with their commonalities at various group levels and proceed to specific discussions of the individual species.

The large number found beside the species' name in its individual discussion corresponds to its photograph in the Photographic Identification section, pages 1-64, and are provided to aid the reader in moving between text and photograph.

Phylum: Porifera

The Sponges

Sponges are a common, oft-times inconspicuous, group of invertebrates living almost exclusively in marine waters. As adults they attach themselves to solid surfaces and are sedentary, virtually motionless, except for the expansion and contraction of pore openings. Some sponges stand erect and have definite shape, appearing like fingers or vases, while others are encrusting, spreading themselves irregularly over rock or shell surfaces. Their colors range through the shades of gray, green, yellow, purple, red and orange, and while some species have one characteristic color, others do not.

Sponges are simple, multicellular animals. Their cells are not organized into tissues or organs as are those of more advanced animals. Although their internal systems vary from one to another, all sponges have one or more large excurrent openings, called oscula, and numerous small incurrent openings, called ostia. A system of canals, sometimes with associated chambers, connects these openings, and the beating of tiny, whiplike flagella draws water through the canals. Food particles entering the sponge with the inflowing water are absorbed and digested.

The taxonomy, or classification, of sponges is derived from

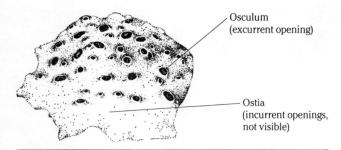

Figure 1. An encrusting sponge. Ostia (incurrent openings) are not visible.

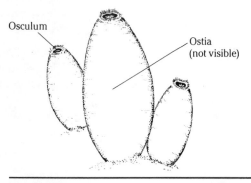

Figure 2. Erect sponges. Osti (incurrent openings) are not visible.

the nature of their supporting skeletons. The skeletons of some sponges, such as those harvested and used commercially, consist largely, or exclusively, of a fibrous, organic material called spongin. In some sponges, however, the primary (and often only) skeletal framework consists of spicules, which are microscopic, calcareous or siliceous crystals. Spicules are found in many shapes; some resemble slender needles, small anchors or sets of jaws.

There are four classes of sponges: the Calcarea, with calcareous spicules; the Hexactinellida, with siliceous spicules that are usually six-rayed; the Demospongiae, whose skeletons contain spongin and/or siliceous spicules that are not six-rayed; and the Sclerospongia, with skeletons of siliceous spicules, organic fibers and crystalline aragonite. The first three classes are represented in Alaskan waters; the Sclerospongia are found in only a few tropical areas.

Identifying a spicule-bearing sponge often requires determining the kind, size and arrangement of the spicules. The sponge's general form, color and size characteristics are also useful in identifying the species, particularly if the appearance of the species is not highly variable and if similar species are not found in the same area.

Sponges can reproduce sexually or asexually. In sexual reproduction, sperm are released from one sponge, carried by water currents to another of the same species, and united with eggs. A fertilized egg usually developes into a tiny larva that emerges from the parent, swims for a time, then settles to the bottom to develop into an adult. Asexual reproduction is by budding, the separation of a piece of the parent sponge. Under favorable conditions, the severed piece grows to form a new individual.

In Alaskan waters sponges are abundant both in species and number. Most species are subtidal, but several encrusting sponges, and a few upright ones, can be found in intertidal zones. The encrusting sponges are often inconspicuous, frequently growing on the underside of rocks, outcroppings or in crevices. A few of the subtidal Alaskan sponges living in rocky areas at depths of 65 meters (36 fathoms) or more are massive, reaching a height and diameter of 1 meter (3.2 feet). Intertidal species tolerate exposure to air; subtidal species soon die if removed from the water.

1 *Scypha compressa*

Height to about 5 centimeters (2 inches). Form is variable — may be elongated and vaselike, or convoluted and ribbonlike. Texture of exterior is roughened by protruding calcareous spicules. Usually gray-white.

Widely distributed, occurring in Alaska from the Aleutian Islands through Southeastern Alaska. Usually subtidal but occasionally intertidal.

2 *Scypha ciliata*

Height to about 10 centimeters (4 inches). Vaselike, with a single, large excurrent opening surrounded by a fringe of long calcareous spicules; surface roughened by protruding spicules. White.

Found worldwide except for Antarctica with probably a wide distribution in Alaska. Usually subtidal, but sometimes small specimens occur intertidally. In Puget Sound, it is known as the "dock sponge" because of its common occurrence on docks, floats and similar structures.

3   *Geodinella robusta*

Diameter to 13 centimeters (5 inches) or more; massive. Shape is irregular, often like a rounded, oblong cushion. Surface is smooth, usually rather uneven, with small, rounded tubercles (knobs). Some areas of its surface have long, protruding spicules. Light brown or light yellow.

From southern California to at least Southeastern Alaska. May grow like a shelf out of a vertical rock face. Often has a covering of microscopic organisms and detritus (organic debris) adhering to the protruding spicules.

4   *Tetilla* sp.

Diameter to about 9 centimeters (3½ inches). Spherical; in size and shape resembles a tennis ball; spicules radiating from the center of the sphere may be as long as 2 centimeters (¾ inch), and form a thick, external "plush." Gray.

Occurs from at least Southeastern Alaska to Amchitka Island in the Aleutian Islands. Subtidal from about 15 meters (8 fathoms) to deep water. Often with microscopic organisms or detritus adhering to the external spicules. The two species of *Tetilla* encountered in Alaskan waters are *T. spinosa*, which has spicules grouped in bundles at its surface, and *T. villosa*, which has spicules evenly distributed at the surface.

5   *Penares cortius*

An irregular encrusting species. May form patches to 30.5 centimeters (12 inches) in diameter. Lump-shaped or cushionlike. Surface smooth, with a definite and distinguishable surface layer; with visible areas of oscula. Texture soft to dense. Usually pale gray, sometimes light brown.

Recorded in the waters of northern California and Southeastern Alaska.

6   *Polymastia* sp.

An irregularly spreading, encrusting sponge. Has upright

thumblike expansions that may measure up to 3.2 centimeters (1¼ inches) in height; each upright expansion has a large, terminal excurrent opening. Yellow to tan.

At least from the Pribilof Islands to Southeastern Alaska. Subtidal. Detritus often covers the encrusting portion of the sponge, leaving only the upright fingers projecting from a darkened surface. The specimen in the photo on page 3 has two kinds of amphipods resting on it.

7 *Mycale lingua*

Diameter to about 25.4 centimeters (10 inches) and thickness to about 10 centimeters (4 inches). Shape varies from nearly spherical to elongate or branching; surface is undulated, roughened, and often with a warty appearance. Yellow-white to brown.

From the Aleutian Islands to Puget Sound. Subtidal. Flabby to the touch; falls apart when taken out of the water. Another species of the genus, *M. adhaerens*, is light brown to violet and often encrusts the valves of live scallops of the genus *Chlamys*.

8 *Myxilla incrustans*

An encrusting species that spreads irregularly over hard surfaces. May also occur as a nonencrusting, massive, and amorphous growth measuring to about 9 centimeters (3½ inches) in diameter. Texture is firm and tough; surface is rough, often with wartlike protuberances. Excurrent openings are large, to 0.6 centimeter (¼ inch) diameter, and sometimes raised on conical outgrowths. Various shades of yellow-gold.

From the Arctic Ocean to southern California. Intertidal and subtidal to 2,500 meters (1,367 fathoms). Intertidally, it tends to be encrusting and massive; subtidally, it often encrusts the valves of live scallops of the genus *Chlamys*. Very similar in appearance to the encrusting *Halichondria*, and only an examination of spicules will distinguish the two. *Mycale adhaerens*, which also occurs on scallop shells, is similar but has more numerous, smaller oscula than *Myxilla incrustans*.

9 *Cliona celata* — Boring Sponge

Without definite shape or size. Bores into live or dead shells, coralline algae, or limestone, creating subcircular tunnels to about 2 millimeters diameter; proliferates out of the tunnels in masses which may be 1 centimeter in diameter; excurrent openings minute; surface smooth but uneven and irregular; yellow.

From California to at least Prince William Sound. Low intertidal and subtidal. Frequently found on large barnacles or bivalves; especially common on large, live rock scallops, *Hinnites multirugosus*. The sponge slows the growth of the organism into which it is boring and may kill it. This species also occurs on the east coast of North America where it is a problem in commercial oyster beds.

10 *Suberites ficus*

Diameter to 10 centimeters (4 inches) or more. A globular, irregular mass; dense, often rubberlike. Orange-red to tan.

From California to at least Unalaska in the Aleutian Islands. Subtidal. May grow independently, but is most often associated with any of several species of hermit crabs. The sponge grows on the snail shell in which the hermit crab lives, increasing in size and simultaneously dissolving the shell. In time, the shell disappears completely, leaving the hermit crab to live in the cavity in the sponge. If the sponge becomes too large and heavy, the hermit crab may abandon it.

11 *Isodictya* sp.

Height to 30.5 centimeters (12 inches) or more. Usually fingerlike, but variable in form. Has numerous, large excurrent openings; terminal openings of fingerlike specimens resemble a bundle of tubes. Surface texture is rough and the sponge is rigid. Usually tan, although occasionally yellow to red.

From the Pribilof Islands to Southeastern Alaska and perhaps farther south. Subtidal. In some areas it is often washed ashore. What is probably another species of *Isodictya* occurs subtidally in the Aleutian Islands — most notable are the specimens that are red, funnel-shaped, and as much as 45.7 centimeters (18 inches) high.

12 *Halichondria panicea*

Usually irregular and encrusting, but may be globular and

25.4 centimeters (10 inches) or more thick; if encrusting, may form a thin layer about 0.6 centimeter (¼ inch) thick, or may be more massive. Surface is rough and irregular. Texture is firm. Has many, small incurrent openings; excurrent openings are few, large, and atop conical or tubular projections that rise about 0.6 centimeter (¼ inch) above the general surface level if the sponge forms a thin encrustation. On more massive growths, excurrent openings often occur atop much taller projections. Color is dull yellow, but where exposed to light may appear green because of the presence of symbiotic algae.

From the Bering Sea to California. Usually low intertidal but may be subtidal as well. Often found on sides of boulders or on bedrock. It is sometimes called the "crumb-of-bread" sponge because of its texture.

Phylum: Cnidaria

The Hydrozoans, Scyphozoans and Anthozoans

Members of the phylum Cnidaria, or Coelenterata as they are also called, are the simplest marine animals with cells arranged in groups of tissues. In form, the cnidarians may be either medusae (like jellyfish) or polyps (like anemones). The medusae are gelatinous, free-swimming invertebrates whose edges are fringed with tentacles. They are hemispherical in shape, convex above and concave below, with a mouth in the center of the lower side. Polyps are not free-swimming but are usually attached to a firm surface. Generally, they have an erect, columnar body with one or more rings of tentacles surrounding a central mouth on the upper surface of the column. While some species of cnidarians alternate between the medusae and polyp forms, others are exclusively polypoid or medusoid.

Cnidarians do not possess circulatory, excretory or respiratory systems; they do, however, have a nervous system. The body cavity is an open area with only a mouth leading to it, through which food is taken in and digested. Undigested residues are expelled from the cavity through the mouth.

Both the medusae and polyps have nematocysts, or stinging capsules, in their tentacles. When stimulated, microscopic threads or darts are released from the nematocysts to entangle or pierce prey or predators. Cnidarians are primarily carnivores, feeding on zooplankton, fish, crustaceans and other cnidarians. Tentacles quickly close around stunned prey, bending it inward to the cnidarian's mouth.

Cnidarians may be solitary (jellyfish and most anemones), social (some anemones) or colonial (many of the hydroids and corals). Many of the colonial forms are so small that a microscope may be needed to identify them and to appreciate their complexity.

Most groups of cnidarians are well represented in Alaskan waters. Surprisingly, even various corals are present, although the reef-building corals found in most tropical waters are not.

Class Hydrozoa — Hydroids, Jellyfishes (Hydromedusae) and Hydrocorals

Most hydrozoan species include both medusa and polyp forms in their life history, and more often than not, the polyp form predominates. The polyp is permanently attached to a firm surface and typically buds off free-swimming medusae, or jellyfish. These medusae reproduce sexually and their motile larvae eventually settle to the bottom to develop into polyps.

Individual hydrozoan polyps are usually tiny and often appear like single anemones. Each has a ring of tentacles with stinging nematocysts around a central mouth. In some species the polyps are solitary and stationed atop long, slender stalks.

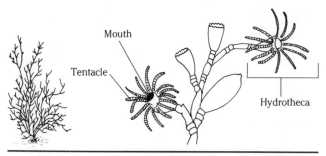

Figure 3. Colonial hydrozoans, called hydrocorals, showing the entire colony and an enlarged view of a portion of the colony.

In other species the polyps grow in colonies, often forming branching networks that have the appearance of delicate plants. The colonial hydrozoans, called hydrocorals, form hard skeletons with starshaped openings, each of which houses several polyps. Most colonial species include two kinds of individuals; those that secure food for the colony, and those that produce medusae. The feeding hydroid polyps, like anemones, pull captured food into a central stomach cavity. The distinctive reproductive polyps are usually shaped like vases or clubs, and depending upon their species, their tiny medusae are either released to the surrounding water or remain with the parent colony to produce another polyp generation.

Hydrozoan medusae differ in several ways from, the medusae of another group, the Scyphozoa. First, hydromedusae are usually smaller, often less than 10 centimeters (4 inches) in diameter. They also possess a velum, a thin membranous shelf that extends inward from the lower edge of the bell. Further, the mouth of a hydromedusa hangs downward on a stalk and is not frilled nor lobed, as is a mouth of a scyphozoan medusa. Hydromedusae reproduce sexually with sperm shed by the male drifting to the female. Tiny ciliated larvae are set free from the female and in time attach to solid surfaces to develop new polyps.

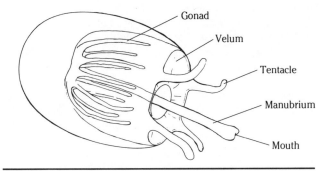

Figure 4. Hydromedusa

The hydrozoans are divided into several orders. Members of Hydroidia — the hydroids — usually have free, or attached but degenerate, medusae in their life histories, but the polyp stage dominates. Members of Hydrocorallina — the hydrocorals — have medusae that are never released from the polyp colonies. Other orders of hydrozoans include floating colonies of polyps and medusae, free floating polyps, or species that produce no polyps at all.

Hydroids

13 *Corymorpha* sp.

Height to about 7 centimeters (2¾ inches). Each polyp is solitary and borne on a long, slender stalk. About 40 basal tentacles form a single circle and reach beyond the end of the polyp. Oral tentacles are numerous and delicate. Gonophores, which bud off to produce the medusoid generation, are present in abundance on branched stalks located immediately in front of the basal tentacles.

Found in Norton Sound. Subtidal. Located on soft surfaces. The specimen in the photograph on page 5 may be *Corymorpha carnea,* the only species of *Corymorpha* described from Norton Sound.

14 *Tubularia* sp.

Height of colony to as much as 30.5 centimeters (12 inches) but usually less; polyps are borne on long, usually unbranched, and often crooked stalks; polyps are large, with two sets of tentacles, the oral tentacles being shorter than the basal ones. The reproductive gonophores are clustered, attached by peduncles — stalklike structures — and lie just ahead of the basal tentacles. Usually orange-red to pink.

Tubularia, which is represented by several species in Alaskan waters, has been reported from Norton Sound to Southeastern Alaska but is not found frequently or in abundance.

15 ? *Campanularia* sp.

Members of the genus *Campanularia* form colonies in which the individual, feeding polyps are borne on stalks that arise from creeping, threadlike stolons. The hard covering on the stalks that support the polyps may be smooth, twisted, or ringed; the hydrotheca (the "goblet" that protects each feeding polyp) is usually bell-shaped.

Often found living on large kelp fronds. Most species do not produce free-swimming medusae. The specimen shown on page 5 was on kelp at a depth of about 10 meters (5.5 fathoms).

16 Family Sertulariidae

A large family. Several genera, including *Abietinaria* and *Sertularella,* occur in Alaskan waters. Microscopic examination is required to determine species and even genus. Members of the family are distinguished by colonies that are usually pinnately branched or treelike. The hydrothecae that cover the feeding polyps are without stalks and are usually arranged in two rows along the main stem and branches of the colony.

The specimen on page 5 was growing at about 10 meters (5.5 fathoms) on a rocky surface. It measured about 7.6 centimeters (3 inches) high and was pale yellow.

17 ? *Aglaophenia* sp.

Colony height to about 25.4 centimeters (10 inches). Appearance is featherlike. Polyps are arranged on one side of each branch off the main stem; reproductive polyps are borne in corbulae (basketlike structures) that appear as lighter, thicker masses along the branches of the colony. Coppery orange.

Occurs in Alaska in exposed coastal areas from Southeastern Alaska to the Aleutian Islands. Medusae of *Aglaophenia* never leave the parent colony; they produce eggs and sperm *in situ.* The larvae escape to form new colonies.

18 *Obelia* sp.

Colony height to about 30.5 centimeters (12 inches) or more. The colony is composed of many delicate, supple and slender branches. Hydrothecae (the cups surrounding the polyps) have thin, translucent walls. Off-white to tan or yellow in color.

At least 5 species of *Obelia* occur in Alaskan waters. They are reported from Southeastern Alaska to Yakutat and Unalaska, but records are incomplete. *Obelia* attaches to firm surfaces. Docks, buoy lines and similar surfaces are often densely covered by its growth. Reproductive polyps of most species produce free-swimming medusae.

Jellyfishes (Hydromedusae)

19   *Staurophora mertensii*

Diameter of bell to 20.3 centimeters (8 inches) or more. Bell is wider than high, with hundreds of short tentacles around the margin. Velum is narrow. Four radial canals form a cross extending nearly to the margin of the bell. Gonads are located along the canals. Mouth has 4 long arms and folded, marginal lips. Radial canals and gonads are white to blue; marginal tentacles are occasionally tinged with pink; the remainder of medusa is transparent with a tinge of blue.

Circumpolar, occuring at least as far south as Puget Sound. Occasionally washed ashore in large numbers. Young specimens swarm at the water's surface; adults are found 1 meter (3.3 feet) or more below the surface. The species has a rapid growth rate and the medusae are some of the largest among the hydrozoans.

20   ? *Calycopsis nematophora*

Height of bell to about 3.2 centimeters (1¼ inches), much taller than it is wide. Four radial canals arise from the top of the manubrium (the stalk on which the mouth is located), then divide into lateral branches that extend downward to the margin of the bell. Gonads are found on the upper part of the manubrium. Oral lobes are located on the lower part of manubrium. The margin of the bell has tentacles varying in number and size. Each radial canal has an associated tentacle. Each tentacle terminates in a nematocyst-bearing knob. The bell is translucent; the manubrium and gonads, pink; oral lobes, yellow-white.

Found in Aleutian Islands and the Bering Sea. The polyp stage of *Calycopsis* is unknown.

21   *Polyorchis penicillatus*

Height of bell to about 6.4 centimeters (2½ inches); width of bell about two-thirds its height. Each of four radial canals has 15-25 pairs of short, dead-end branches extending outward at right angles. Usually with 10 or more slender gonads on each radial canal. Up to 160 tentacles arranged in 2-4 rows around the margin of the bell. A red eyespot is present at the base of each tentacle. The manubrium is about as long as the bell cavity. The bell is transparent; radial canals, gonads and manubrium are opaque white; tentacles are pink-orange.

From the Gulf of California to as far north as Southeastern Alaska.

22 *Eperetmus typus*

Width of bell to about 2.5 centimeters (1 inch); height slightly more than one-half width; has 4 radial canals and additional short, dead-end canals that arise by bell margin. Tentacles vary in size; more numerous than the marginal canals. Oral lips crenulated (scalloped); each bears a row of nematocyst bulbs. The bell is transparent; radial canals and manubrium are translucent white; tentacles are tinged with pale pink.

From Puget Sound to as far north as Southeastern Alaska.

23 ? *Eutonina indicans*

Diameter of bell to about 3.8 centimeters (1½ inches); has 4 unbranched, radial canals. Elongate gonads are located on radial canals. Has more than 100 close-set, identical tentacles. Bell transparent; manubrium and gonads are milky white.

Around Unalaska Island, Puget Sound, and California to depths of 20 meters (10.9 fathoms); abundant in protected bays in concentrations of a hundred or more per cubic foot.

24 *Aequorea* sp.

Diameter of bell to about 17.8 centimeters (7 inches). The bell is saucer-shaped, thick in the center and thinning toward margin. Radial canals may number 100 or more. Gonads are located along the radial canals. The number of tentacles is variable but may exceed the number of radial canals. Manubrium usually appears off-center. The bell is transparent; radial canals and manubrium are translucent white.

Aequorea aequorea, probably the most common species, is found from the Bering Sea and the Aleutian Islands to Puget Sound, and perhaps to Baja California. Luminescent.

25 *Solmissus* sp.

Diameter of bell to about 5 centimeters (2 inches). The bell is flattened and much wider than it is tall. About 16 tentacles rise from above the margin of the bell. Transparent.

Species of *Solmissus* occur in Puget Sound and northward to the Bering Sea. Not well documented in Alaska.

Hydrocorals

26 *Allopora campyleca*

Colonies to about 10 centimeters (4 inches) or more in height. Branching is irregular and in more than one plane. The starlike concavities that house the soft polyps are usually well separated from one another, but occasionally are almost connected; concavities are arranged irregularly on the stems and branches of the colony, but are more numerous on the front and sides than on the rear of the colony. Pale pink to white.

Members of the genus *Allopora* occur in Alaskan waters from the Aleutian Islands to the southeastern sector. They are generally not common, but may be locally abundant and usually grow in areas of moderate tidal current. Colonies are picked up on longline fishing gear and boat anchors dropped on rock-rubble bottoms. The specimen shown on page 8 may be the subspecies *A. campyleca paragea,* which has been reported from Southeastern Alaska to Yakutat.

27 *Stylantheca porphyra*

Colony is encrusting, thin and irregular. The skeleton is calcareous, hard and often with small papillae. Soft polyps live in star-shaped concavities in the hard skeleton. Pink to purple.

From California to Southeastern Alaska. Subtidal, but occasionally intertidal. The specimen in the photograph on page 8 has overgrown the shells of several barnacles.

Class Scyphozoa — Jellyfishes
(Scyphomedusae)

Most scyphozoans, like the hydrozoans, alternate polyp and medusa generations. Among scyphozoans, however, the medusa stage is prominent, while the polyps are generally small and inconspicuous. Scyphozoan medusae are larger than those of the hydrozoans, usually more than 10 centimeters (4 inches) in diameter, and they lack a velum. The mouths of most scyphozoan medusae found in Alaskan waters have four frilly lobes, and the gonads are often horseshoe-shaped and found in pouches off the stomach.

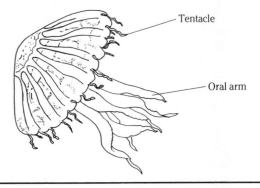

Figure 5. Scyphomedusa

The scyphozoan polyp, called a scyphistoma, is usually vaselike and topped with tentacles that trap food and bring it to the central mouth. When conditions are right, the scyphistomae divide into a stack of lobed, saucerlike disks. These disks are set free and develop into medusae. Because of their small size, scyphozoan polyps are easily overlooked. They are abundant, however, on solid, subtidal surfaces.

Scyphozoan medusae, like other cnidarians, have nematocysts for the capture of food and protection. These nematocysts, however, can deliver a wallop, and the unwary diver, fisherman or beachcomber who inadvertently comes in contact with the tentacles of some scyphomedusae may still feel their stinging effect several hours later. It is curious to note, however, that in spite of the potency of the nematocysts, some small fishes and crustaceans are found in close association with large jellyfish, apparently deriving protection as they swim unaffected beneath the bell and among the tentacles. In Alaska, for example, young pollock live near the large jellyfish *Cyanea capillata,* darting among its tentacles and under its bell when disturbed.

Reproduction among scyphozoans is usually sexual in the medusa generation and asexual budding in the polyp generation. Some species by-pass the polyp stage, with medusa-stage reproduction leading directly to more medusae.

Most scyphozoans found in Alaskan waters belong to the Semaestomeae, a group characterized in part by scalloped bell margins and mouths with four frilly lobes. Another, somewhat smaller group is the Stauromedusae, whose members attach themselves to algae or other objects by a stalked, adhesive pad extending from the animal's aboral surface. The upper end of the stalk expands into a disk resembling an inside-out umbrella. The disk's center bears a mouth on a short manubrium. The edge of the oral surface is drawn into lobes, the tips of which bear short densely clustered tentacles. The gonads extend like spokes from the mouth area to the tips of the lobes. Stauromedusae are sub-tidal, and while uncommon in Alaska, their unique form and occasional abundance make them noteworthy.

28   *Aurelia labiata*

Diameter of bell to about 30.5 centimeters (12 inches). Bell is generally low and flattened, and the margin is divided by clefts into 16 lobes (8 primary lobes, each notched once). Canals are numerous and branch profusely near the margin of the bell. Sense organs are borne in shallow clefts. Tentacles are numerous and short. The oral lobes are fairly short, thick and somewhat folded in appearance. The 4 gonads are horseshoe-shaped, and the open end of each faces the center of the bell. Bell is translucent with a yellow to blue tinge.

Widespread from California to Southeastern Alaska and may well be found farther north and south. It is one of the more common, large jellyfishes in Alaskan waters, especially in Southeastern Alaska during the summer and fall. *A. labiata* serves as food for the jellyfish *Cyanea capillata*, for green urchins, the crab *Hyas lyratus*, and for burrowing anemones. *A. aurita* is a similar species, but it has a margin divided into 8 primary lobes without secondary divisions. *A. limbata*, a species found in the Bering Sea and Aleutian Islands, is similar to *A. labiata* but its light, translucent bell has a dark edge.

29   *Phacellophora camtschatica*

Width of bell to about 61 centimeters (24 inches). Margin of bell has 16 large, rounded lobes that alternate with smaller lobes; each smaller lobe bears a sense organ. Tentacles are arranged in 16 linear clusters of up to 25 tentacles each; tentacles arise from the underside of the marginal lobes. Gonads are protrusive and sacklike. Oral lobes are extensively frilled. Bell is transparent.

From the Bering Sea to Chile.

30 *Chrysaora melanaster*

Diameter of bell to about 30.5 centimeters (12 inches) or more; height about one-third width. Marginal lobes are of almost equal size and shape. With 8 marginal sense organs that alternate with single rows of 3-5 long, thick tentacles. Oral arms are long, pointed and folded in appearance. The bell is translucent to opaque, with 32 red or brown radiating streaks on its upper surface and 16 dark, radiating streaks on its underside.

From the Aleutian and Pribilof islands to California. This species is food for the anemone *Tealia crassicornis*.

31 *Cyanea capillata* — Lion's Mane Jellyfish

Diameter of bell to 50.8 centimeters (20 inches) or more. Bell is generally flattened and thick in the center, thin at the margin. Margin is divided into 8 deep lobes, which are in turn divided by a shallow cleft. A sense organ is located in each shallow cleft. Has several hundred tentacles, which may be 9 meters (29.5 feet) or longer when fully extended, and four long, oral lobes with folded edges. Translucent to opaque, red-brown to yellow; large individuals are sometimes white.

From Point Barrow to as far south as California. This jellyfish is sometimes abundant locally, and may foul fishing gear. It serves as a host for juvenile fish, such as pollock, and for amphipods. It feeds on virtually anything its tentacles touch and hold, including the nudibranch *Melibe leonina* and other jellyfish such as *Aurelia labiata*. It falls prey to burrowing anemones, the crab *Hyas lyratus*, shrimp, nudibranchs, and the anemone *Metridium senile. C. capillata* is the jellyfish that most often stings humans in Alaskan waters.

32 *Haliclystus* sp.

Width to about 2.5 centimeters (1 inch). Has well-developed marginal lobes and 8 clusters of terminally knobbed tentacles. Gonads extend to the end of the tentacle-bearing arms. Translucent; gonads white to yellow.

Found in Southeastern Alaska. Subtidal and usually attached to algae or eelgrass. More than one genus of stalked jellyfish occur in Alaskan waters — members of some genera may be larger and more vase-shaped than *Haliclystus.*

Class Anthozoa — Soft Corals, Sea Pens, Sea Whips, Anemones and Their Allies

Anthozoans are strictly polypoid in form without medusoid generations. They may be solitary (most of the anemones), social (some of the anemones) or colonial (sea pens, sea whips and soft corals). In every case, the individual anthozoan polyp consists of a cylindrical column topped by tentacles encircling a central mouth, which leads indirectly to a sacklike stomach through a gullet. The stomach is incompletely divided by partitions projecting inward like spokes from the body wall.

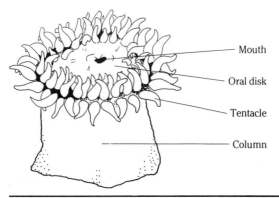

Figure 6. Anemone

Anemones of the order Actinaria are the most common anthozoans in Alaska and are found in intertidal and subtidal zones. When exposed by receding tides, they are limp, shapeless mounds. When supported by sea water, they stand upright and extend their tentacles like flower petals. Anemones feed by drawing food from their tentacles into the mouth. Anemones, like other cnidarians, possess stinging nematocysts, found on the tentacles and sometimes on threadlike structures called acontia. The acontia originate at the free edges of the partitions and are extruded through the mouth or through pores in the body wall. Although capable of use in capturing prey and repelling predators, the nematocysts are too weak to harm humans.

Excluding anemones, most Alaskan anthozoans are members of the colonial group Octocorallia, whose members typically have polyps with eight tentacles and eight internal, stomach partitions. The many polyps in each colony are often supported by a spicule skeleton. Only a few octocorallian species are found in Alaska. Of these, the tall sea pens and sea whips occur in relatively shallow waters; large branching colonies of gorgonians (sea fans) have been taken from deeper areas; soft corals, although less common here than in tropical waters, may occasionally be abundant.

Sexual reproduction among anthozoans usually results in ciliated larvae that swim for a while before settling to the sea floor to develop into adults. Some anthozoans also reproduce asexually with tissue separated from a parent developing into a new individual.

Soft Coral

33 *Gersemia rubiformis*

Height of colony to about 5 centimeters (2 inches). Colony has a broad base and bears dense groups of small polyps. Polyps can retract into the colony. Translucent; usually pale pink.

From the Bering Sea to northern California. Subtidal; low intertidal in southern part of range. Found on small rocks or other hard surfaces. Commonly washed ashore in the Bering Sea and Gulf of Alaska. Reportedly preyed upon by the nudibranch *Tochuina tetraquetra*. A number of other species of soft coral are also found in Alaskan waters.

Sea Pen

34 *Ptilosarcus gurneyi*

Height of colony to about 45.7 centimeters (18 inches). The stalk is fleshy, with a short, internal supporting rod in the lower, buried portion. Polyps are borne on two series of leaflike branches along the upper part of the stalk. Orange.

Occurs from Prince William Sound to California. Subtidal and common at depths of 10-25 meters (5-13.5 fathoms) where there is light to moderate current. May occur to depths of 100 meters (55 fathoms) or more. Found on sand with the lower portion of the central stalk below the surface and serving as an anchor. The colony is capable of retracting into the substrate. And is often preyed upon by a number of nudibranchs.

Sea Whip

35 ? *Virgularia* sp.

Height to about 30.5 centimeters (12 inches). The stalk is long and slender, with an internal supporting rod. Polyps are arranged in transverse rows along the stalk in groups that look like hands; several polyps connect at their bases to a broad, flattened expanse that is in turn attached to the stalk. The lower part of the stalk is widened slightly. White.

Distribution is uncertain. The species occurs in Southeastern Alaska, perhaps south to Puget Sound and farther north as well. Subtidal and found on sand and silt surfaces. The colony does not retract into the bottom. At least 2 other species of sea whip occur in Alaskan waters. They differ from ? *Virgularia* sp. in the arrangement of polyps along the stalk. Some Alaskan species may be 2 meters (6½ feet) or more in total height.

Sea Fan

36 Order Gorgonacea

Height of colonies in photo on page 10 to about 25.4 centimeters (10 inches). Branches primarily in two dimensions. Each colony has a flexible, horny, internal skeleton and a softer, outer layer with spicules. Polyps arise from the outer layer. The softer tissue is pink; internal skeleton, tan.

Specimens shown were found at a depth of about 30 meters (16.4 fathoms) on a rocky prominence and were oriented broadside to the current. Some species reach 2 meters (6½ feet) in height. Most species of gorgonians are found only in deep waters, but some occur as shallow as 9 meters (4.9 fathoms). Species in Alaska are not well known.

Cup Coral

37 *Balanophyllia elegans*

Diameter to about 1.3 centimeters (½ inch) and height about the same. Species looks like a tiny anemone, but has a calcareous skeleton which underlies its outer wall and internal partitions. Bright yellow to yellow-orange.

Occurs from California to northern Southeastern Alaska. Intertidal and subtidal in its southern range. In Alaska it is usually subtidal at 15 meters (8.2 fathoms) or deeper. Although not common, it is abundant where it occurs.

Anemones

38 *Pachycerianthus fimbriatus*

Crown of tentacles to about 20.3 centimeters (8 inches) in diameter. Tentacles are numerous and arranged in 2 groups— a marginal ring of long, slender tentacles, and an inner oral ring of slender, short tentacles. The animal lives in a tough tube of its own construction that extends 1 meter (3.3 feet) or more below the surface. Tentacles are yellow-brown with narrow bands of dark brown, or occasionally solid purple-black.

From California to Southeastern Alaska. Subtidal, but occasionally found in low intertidal zones in its southern range, usually in sand and gravel. This species can retract rapidly into its tube if disturbed. It is preyed upon by the nudibranch *Dendronotus iris.*

39 *Epizoanthus scotinus*

Height to about 5 centimeters (2 inches). The column is light brown to orange or yellow-white; tentacles and the area surrounding the mouth are white to pale orange.

From Puget Sound to the western Aleutian Islands. Subtidal, but intertidal as well in its southern range. Usually found on vertical or overhanging bedrock surfaces. The species is a social anemone — basal material extending from each individual gives rise to new members of the colony. Each colony may be a few to a hundred or more individuals that form a tightly packed, dense mat.

40 *Metridium senile*

Height to about 50.8 centimeters (20 inches) or more. Tentacles are numerous and slender with the inner tentacles being larger than the outer ones; tentacles branch profusely, especially in large specimens; the young have fewer tentacles than adults. The oral disk is larger in diameter than the column; the disk is lobed or scalloped in large specimens. The column is white, orange, pink or brown; tentacles are translucent, usually a lighter shade of the column.

Circumpolar with a southern range to California. Found in low intertidal and subtidal zones to a depth of 100 meters (55 fathoms) or more. Often found on pilings or floats in harbors and bays and is common on bedrock or other hard surfaces in areas of moderate current, such as straits or channels. This organism may live solitarily or in dense beds that totally cover the sea bottom. In addition to sexual reproduction, this species reproduces asexually by separation of a portion of its base. Small specimens feed on relatively large food items, while large individuals feed primarily on small planktonic organisms. *Metridium senile* is one of the largest and most obvious anemones in Alaska.

41 *Tealia crassicornis*

Height to about 30.5 centimeters (12 inches). The column has small tubercles and irregular red and olive markings (occasionally uniform red or brown). Tentacles are encircled with broad, red bands; narrow red lines radiate from mouth on the oral disk or around the bases of the tentacles.

From the Pribilof Islands to California. Intertidal (often on sides of large boulders) and subtidal. This anemone may feed on large organisms such as tanner crabs, hermit crabs, the jellyfish *Cyanea capillata,* sea urchins, chitons, and fish.

42 *Tealia lofotensis*

Height to about 25.4 centimeters (10 inches). The column brilliant red with bright white tubercles that are occasionally arranged in longitudinal rows. The tentacles have crimson tips.

From California to Southeastern Alaska. Subtidal in Alaska, but in southern range also occurs intertidally on vertical rock faces. Shell fragments may adhere to its tubercles.

43   *Cribrinopsis fernaldi*

Height to about 25.4 centimeters (10 inches). The column has small white tubercles arranged in numerous longitudinal rows often restricted to the upper third of the column. The tentacles are long and tapering with numerous transverse irregular red or yellow streaks. The column is usually white or pink, sometimes yellow; the disk is a similar color to the column and occasionally has thin red or yellow lines radiating from the mouth or encircling the tentacle bases.

Occurs from Puget Sound to the Aleutian Islands in subtidal zones to 300 meters (164 fathoms) or deeper. The species is often found on bedrock walls and attached to small rocks or clam shells on sandy mud bottoms. Fertilized eggs brood for about 20 days in the female before larvae are released. *C. fernaldi* is host to various species of hippolytid shrimps living near or on it, especially the brilliantly colored *Lebbeus* sp.

44   *Epiactis* sp.

Height to about 7.6 centimeters (3 inches). The tentacles are thick at the base and taper to the tips. The column is a deep red-orange; the tentacles and oral disk are nearly the same in color.

Occurs in the Bering Sea. In the genus *Epiactis,* larvae develop within the parent, then travel out the parent's mouth and down its side to become attached to the lower part of the stalk. This behavior gives them their common designation as brooding anemones. *E. prolifera,* which has a pink, red, brown, or green column, radiating white lines on the oral disk, and lines on the column base, occurs in shallow water from California to Southeastern Alaska.

45   *Anthopleura xanthogrammica*

Diameter of crown to about 25.4 centimeters (10 inches). The column is green or olive and covered with irregularly arranged tubercles. The tentacles are uniformly green.

From Southeastern Alaska to California. Usually found in subtidal zones in Alaska but occurs in low intertidal zones in its southern range. May be found alone or in groups. Its bright green coloration is caused by symbiotic algae living within the anemone's tissues. If the anemone lives where there is no sunlight, it is pink, lavender, or white.

46 *Anthopleura artemisia*

Diameter of crown to about 5 centimeters (2 inches). Tubercles cover the upper two-thirds of the column. Tentacles are long and slender. The lower two-thirds of the column is white or pink, the upper third being black or gray; tentacles are green, tan, copper, gray or pink with incomplete encircling white bands.

From California to Southeastern Alaska. Intertidal and shallow subtidal. The anemone buries itself partially in sand or shell gravel, attaching itself to a hard object beneath the surface and leaving little more than the oral disk and tentacles exposed. When the anemone withdraws, it leaves a circular indentation in the surface. *Anthopleura artemisia* is a common intertidal anemone in Southeastern Alaska, found in tide pools and sandy areas.

47 *Stomphia coccinea*

Height to about 7.6 centimeters (3 inches) or more. The column may be as wide as it is tall. It has no tubercles. The anemone is orange with a white spot at the base of each tentacle.

From Point Barrow to Washington. Subtidal. If contacted by certain sea stars, this anemone will swim weakly, probably as a means of escape from the potential predator. To swim, the anemone releases its hold on the surface, and bends its column first one way, then another.

Phylum: Ctenophora

The Comb Jellies

Like the jellyfish, ctenophores, or comb jellies, are free-swimming creatures. They differ, however, by their longitudinal bands of combs, each of which is a platelike group of fused cilia that beats to propel the animal through the water. They may possess tentacles, too. Some species have a single pair of long, retractable tentacles arising at mid-body; others have several, short tentacles near the mouth.

Most comb jellies are small, translucent or transparent, and

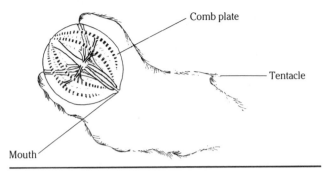

Figure 7. Ctenophore

tinged with pink, orange, violet or olive. The combs are often iridescent.

Although comb jellies are found at considerable ocean depths, they are more abundant near the water surface, where they swim weakly and feed on crustaceans, planktonic larvae, fish eggs and other comb jellies. Their prey is usually captured with the use of adhesive cells, called colloblasts, located on the tentacles or on the body surface. A few species of ctenophores are apparently more aggressive feeders than others and will actively turn their gaping mouths toward potential prey in an attempt to draw them in.

Their lifespan is probably a year or less. They are hermaphroditic and usually expel eggs and sperm through their mouths into the surrounding water where fertilization occurs. The larvae are free-swimming and resemble their parents. Comb jellies display strong regenerative capabilities, being able to replace damaged or lost parts, even to produce a new comb jelly from half a specimen.

Comb jellies are abundant in Alaskan waters and at times occur in great numbers.

48 *Bolinopsis* sp.

Length to about 7.6 centimeters (3 inches). The body is cylindrical or nearly spherical with 2 types of short tentacles near the mouth. The body is divided into 2 large lobes at oral end. The comb bands do not extend the full length of the animal, and 4 are shorter than the others. Translucent.

Species of *Bolinopsis* occur from Point Barrow and the Aleutian Islands to Southeastern Alaska and as far south as California. Feeds on plankton.

49 *Beroe* sp.

Length to about 13 centimeters (5 inches). Body is long, cylindrical, shaped like a cucumber. Mouth is wide and conspicuous. Has no oral tentacles or oral lobes. The canals of the digestive tract branch irregularly, creating a netlike appearance over the animal. Comb bands of equal length taper near mouth and extend most of the length of the animal. Translucent, often with a tinge of pink; combs are iridescent.

Species of *Beroe* are reported from Point Barrow to as far south as California. Along Alaska's coast these animals are seen near the surface, and although not frequently observed, they may be abundant locally when they occur. They may feed on crustaceans and other ctenophores. This species appears to sense movement in nearby water, opening its mouth wide toward any moving object.

50 *Pleurobrachia* sp.

Length of body to about 1.3 centimeters (½ inch); body is spherical to egg-shaped. The tentacles are long, 5 or more times the body length, and retract into a sheath. The comb bands are conspicuous. Transparent and may have a tinge of light red to plum; combs are iridescent.

Species of *Pleurobrachia* are reported from the Arctic Ocean to California; they may be locally abundant in Southeastern Alaska. The tentacles, which are armed with adhesive cells, contract to carry captured prey to the animal's mouth. This animal feeds at least in part on small crustaceans.

Phylum:
Platyhelminthes
The Flatworms

Members of the phylum Platyhelminthes are bilaterally symmetrical animals with a definite head, a brain, and many light-sensitive cells associated with pigmented "eyespots." Most are hermaphroditic and possess complex reproductive systems. Typically, they are flattened from top to bottom.

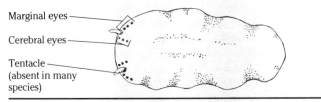

Marginal eyes

Cerebral eyes

Tentacle
(absent in many
species)

Figure 8. A polyclad flatworm, dorsal view

The phylum is divided into several classes, but only one of these, the Turbellaria, includes free-living flatworms. Members of other groups, which include the tapeworms and flukes, are parasites.

The Turbellaria are primarily marine and fresh water animals, and several major groups are represented in the coastal waters of the north Pacific Ocean. Only one order of Turbellaria, the Polycladida, includes worms likely to be noticed without a microscope.

Polyclad flatworms are characterized by a gut with many branches. Most polyclads have numerous eyespots on the anterior portion of their bodies, and a few, but not all, have tentacles arising in the front. The polyclad worms are usually inconspicuously dull in appearance; however, some species have bright colors and striking markings which are, considering that the colors and markings vary within a species, probably due to the worm's diet. Therefore, color is not a useful identification tool.

The polyclads are carnivorous and feed on small worms, molluscs, and crustaceans. The worm's mouth is located mid-body on the creature's underside. A few species possess a pharynx, which can be extended outside the main body through the mouth, allowing digestion to begin externally.

Polyclad worms are both intertidal and subtidal, where they are found in rocky areas hidden among other invertebrates or algae. Polyclads appear to glide over surfaces, a motion accomplished by a musculature system, perhaps aided by cilia. Some polyclads can swim.

Although hermaphroditic, polyclads cross-fertilize. Eggs are laid in flat patches in protected places, such as the undersides of rocks. Free-swimming microscopic larvae are characteristic of some species.

51 Order Polycladida
Length to about 1.9 centimeters (¾ inch). Tentacles are

located just behind the front edge. The body is off-white with a pure white border and numerous irregularly distributed red-brown flecks; tentacles are red.

Specimen shown on page 14 was found subtidally at a depth of about 9 meters (4.9 fathoms) on a sandy, rock-rubble surface.

Phylum: Nemertea

The Ribbon Worms

Nemerteans, or ribbon worms, are slender, somewhat flat worms that primarily exist in intertidal and subtidal marine waters. To a lesser degree, they are found in fresh water and on moist terrain. They are often brightly and distinctively colored and are capable of stretching to great lengths — up to 15 meters (49 feet) in some species. The body of a nemertean is unsegmented, smooth and covered with tiny cilia. To the touch they feel slippery because of a mucus secreted by the worm. The body's anterior end and/or sides usually bear light-sensitive cells associated with "eyespot" pigments (ocelli), and the creature's mouth is located on the underside of the anterior end.

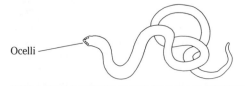

Ocelli

Figure 9. Nemertean

Depending upon the species, ribbon worms are free living, parasitic or commensal. The animal feeds with an eversible proboscis, an expandable, trunklike organ that may be as long as the worm itself. When not in use, the proboscis lies in a fluid-filled cavity within the worm's body. To attack prey, powerful muscles shoot the proboscis through the mouth or other body orifice. Some proboscises are sticky and adhere to stricken prey; others are armed with venomous stylets that penetrate to kill. The captured prey, often an annelid worm, is held in the coil of the retracting proboscis, carried to the ribbon worm's mouth, and usually swallowed whole.

The sexes of nemerteans are usually separate. The few species that are hermaphroditic are incapable of self-fertilization. Eggs and sperm are shed about the same time with fertilization occurring within or outside of the female. Some species bear live young, others deposit gelatinous masses or threads containing eggs.

In marine waters, the ribbon worms are found under or among rocks, beneath fronds of algae, or in mucus tubes they make in muddy or sandy substrates. A number of species are found in the intertidal and subtidal waters of Alaska.

52 *Tubulanus sexlineatus*

Body length to more than 20.3 centimeters (8 inches); may be 1 meter (39 inches) or more in length when fully extended. Has numerous, well-developed sense organs, including some located along the sides of the body. The general color is dull orange to deep brown with 6 longitudinal white lines (each line is actually a series of closely spaced dots); has as many as 150 or more evenly spaced, white rings encircling the body.

From Southeastern Alaska to central California. Lives in a tough, translucent, open-ended tube. Found on pilings or rocks, among algae or mussels.

Phylum: Mollusca

The Amphineurans, Gastropods, Bivalves and Cephalopods

Because of their size, beauty, abundance and commercial importance, molluscs are, as a whole, better known and studied than are members of most marine phyla. The molluscs species share several characteristics, despite their being such a diverse group of animals. Their soft bodies are unsegmented and they usually have a definite head equipped with special sense organs. Part of the body wall may grow out around the animal to form a mantle. Their digestive, circulatory and nervous systems are well developed. Their ventral sides usually possess a muscular foot, the animals' means of locomotion. Finally, many, but not all, molluscs, are protected by a hard shell with one or more valves. The shell may be external, internal, or exist only in the earliest stages of the animal's development.

There are thousands of marine molluscan species, and in Alaskan waters many can be found from the high intertidal zone to great depths. Some are pelagic, others live on the ocean floor, and still others burrow into sand, mud, rubble or the wood of logs, docks and pilings.

The four major groups of molluscs are: Amphineura (chitons), Gastropoda (limpets, snails and nudibranchs), Bivalvia (clams, mussels and cockles) and Cephalopoda (octopuses and squids). All are commonly found in Alaska's shallow marine waters.

To identify a molluscan species one must contend with varying characteristics. If the animal has a shell, identification is usually based on its form; however, for some shell-bearing molluscs, such as the limpets, the microscopic examination of the radula, or feeding structure, may be important. If the mollusc has no shell, or if the shell is small and internal, the identification must be based on the animal's soft body.

Class Amphineura — Chitons

Chitons, the most familiar members of the class Amphineura, belong to the subclass Polyplacophora, the "bearers of many plates." They have a distinctive shell that consists of eight, overlapping plates, or valves, arranged in a longitudinal row on the dorsal surface. In most chitons, the plates are clearly visible, but in a few, they are completely covered by tissue. Only the plates and the surrounding girdle are visible on the animal's dorsal surface. On the ventral side, the girdle, the foot, and the mouth, at the anterior end between the foot and girdle, are visible. The chiton is shallow and flat, making it well suited for adhering to rocky surfaces of surf and surge.

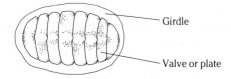

Girdle

Valve or plate

Figure 10. Chiton, dorsal view

Some chitons are active during the day, but many feed at night, withdrawing by day to the undersides of rocks. An active chiton feeds by scraping algae and detritus from rocks with its radula. Many chitons graze over restricted areas, and then return to a specific spot.

The sexes in chitons are separate, and, in most cases, the eggs are deposited externally, the female releasing them after nearby males shed their sperm.

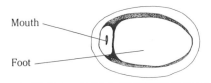

Mouth

Foot

Figure 11. Chiton, ventral view

53 *Tonicella lineata*

Length to about 5 centimeters (2 inches). The central area of intermediate plates is a solid color, often pink to deep red; lateral areas usually have the same color as background, but are marked by dark, wavering lines bordered by white or pale blue; end plates have concentric lines of the same color, variations in the color pattern may occur on individual plates. The girdle is smooth, with a mottled coloration.

From the Bering Sea and Aleutian Islands to southern California. Intertidal and shallow subtidal. Common on rocky surfaces. The young live offshore and migrate inshore as they mature.

54 *Tonicella insignis*

Length to about 3.8 centimeters (1½ inches). The end plates and lateral areas of intermediate plates are rose- to maroon-red; the central areas of the intermediate plates are a deeper red marked by wavering, transverse white lines; the anterior edge of the tail plate and the posterior margin of all plates have a narrow band that repeats the pattern of the central area of the intermediate plates. The girdle is smooth and often red marked by irregular, light blotches, a narrow band at the outer edge of the girdle is overlain with translucent green.

From Kodiak Island to Washington. Shallow subtidal.

55 *Mopalia lignosa*

Length to about 6.4 centimeters (2½ inches). The plates are a dull, dark green, or cream to greenish white with dark, feathery markings. The plate sculpture is delicate, sometimes pitted near the center. The girdle is a solid color or marked with brown and yellow; it has short, broad hairs. The plates are green-white to white on the inside.

From Baja California to Southeastern Alaska. Lower intertidal and shallow subtidal.

56 *Mopalia muscosa*

Length to about 5 centimeters (2 inches). The head plate has 10 beaded, radial ribs; intermediate plates are flat-sided with a central area of curving, longitudinal sculpturing. The girdle has a dense covering of stiff, long hair and a small, shallow notch at its posterior end. The plates and girdle are dull brown, green or gray; plates are blue-green on the inside.

From Baja California to Southeastern Alaska. Shallow subtidal.

57 *Placiphorella rufa*

Length to about 3.2 centimeters (1¼ inches). Outline is oval. The anterior plate is crescent-shaped with strong, irregular growth lines and weak, radial grooves; intermediate plates have ribs in lateral areas; posterior plate is small, about one-half as wide as the anterior plate. The girdle is much broader at its anterior end and smooth, except for minute spines along the edge and 3-4 series of stiff, hairlike projections. The girdle is buff; plates, red-brown.

From British Columbia and Southeastern Alaska to perhaps the Aleutian Islands. Subtidal to at least 45 meters (24.6 fathoms). It traps prey under its girdle, which is held above the substrate when the animal is not disturbed. *P. velata* is similar but has a red-yellow girdle and plates that are olive-brown with streaks of tan, blue, pink, or brown. Three other species of *Placiphorella* are recorded in Alaskan waters.

58 *Katharina tunicata* — Gum Boot, Black Leather Chiton

Length to 7.6 centimeters (3 inches) or more. A shiny black

girdle covers two-thirds of each plate; the exposed plate area is gray-black; the inside of the plates and external, covered portions are white.

From the Aleutian Islands to southern California. Intertidal and shallow subtidal. A traditional food for many Alaskan Natives.

59   *Cryptochiton stelleri* — Gum Boot, Chinese Slipper

Length to about 30 centimeters (12 inches) or more. Plates white, shaped like butterflies and completely covered by a thick, tough, red-brown girdle; surface of girdle roughened by minute spines.

From the Pribilof and Aleutian Islands to southern California. Low intertidal and shallow subtidal. Usually found on rock. It is the largest chiton in the world.

Class Gastropoda — Limpets, Abalone, Snails, Nudibranchs and Their Allies

Nearly three-fourths of all molluscs are gastropods. They are a diverse group — some have obvious shells, others have none; some are strictly marine, others live on land and have lunglike structures. Among those with obvious shells, the shape, size, color and surface texture of the shell vary from species to species, creating an amazing array of designs.

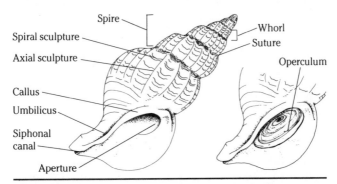

Figure 12. Characteristics of a gastropod shell

All gastropods are asymmetrical and at some point in their development have a characteristic spiral shell. Their heads are better developed than those of chitons and bivalves and usually bear both tentacles and eyes. Feeding is by use of a radula. Most gastropods have a mantle and use a large, flat, ventral foot for locomotion. Species with a spirally-coiling shell usually can retreat into the shell for protection; some also close the shell opening with an operculum, a chitinous or calcareous plate on the dorsal surface of the foot.

Most gastropods with obvious external shells belong to the subclass Prosobranchia. Limpets and abalones, two of the primitive prosobranchs, have low, caplike shells and radulae to scrape algae and detritus off rocks. Advanced prosobranchs, such as the whelks and olives, may be specialized carnivores with correspondingly specialized radulae. In some, the radula and associated structures drill into the shells of barnacles or molluscs; in others a large radular tooth injects venom into prey.

Opisthobranchs, a second subclass of gastropods, often lack shells. They include the nudibranchs, or sea slugs. These animals may be inconspicuously translucent or opaque, or bright with color, stripes and spots. Nudibranchs breathe through feathery structures or directly through the body surface. As a group they have diverse diets, but individual species may be selective in their choice of food. (Some feed exclusively on cnidarians and store ingested nematocysts in soft cerata as protection against predators.)

The third group of gastropods, the Pulmonata, are air-

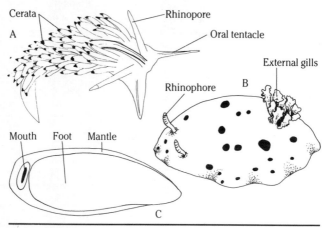

Figure 13. Two forms of nudibranchs (A and B) and the ventral view (C).

breathers. Most live on land or in fresh water, but a few species are found in marine waters.

Pulmonates and opisthobranchs are usually hermaphroditic. The latter lay eggs in a gelatinous matrix extruded from the parent animal in spirals. In prosobranchs, the sexes are usually separate. The more primitive prosobranchs usually spawn free floating eggs. Among more advanced species of prosobranchs, eggs may be laid by the female in capsules she attaches to the substrate. Among most gastropod species, larvae emerge from the eggs and live pelagically for a brief period before metamorphosing into adults and settling to the sea floor.

Limpets

60 *Acmaea mitra*

Length of shell to about 3.8 centimeters (1½ inches); height up to three-fourths the length. Conical. The margin is nearly circular and the apex erect. Shell is white, inside and out.

From the Pribilof and Aleutian islands to Baja California. Low intertidal and shallow subtidal. *A. mitra* feeds on coralline algae, like that which often covers its shell. Some corallines found on *A. mitra,* including the one in the photograph on page 17, have a knobby growth.

61 *Collisella digitalis*

Length of shell to about 3.8 centimeters (1½ inches). The apex is one-third or less of the shell length from the anterior end. Anterior slope is usually concave, other slopes convex. Has widely spaced, strong radial ribs. The shell exterior is gray to olive, or brown, with irregular white bands or mottling. The margin of the shell interior is dark, or dark with white; apex interior is dark brown; intermediate area, white.

From Unimak Island to Baja California. Upper intertidal zone. Often found in crevices. The broad radial ribs of this limpet distinguish it from *Notoacmaea persona,* which also occurs in the upper intertidal zone.

62 *Notoacmea scutum*

Length of shell to 6.4 centimeters (2½ inches); height is one-fourth length or less. The shell is conical, low and flattened. All slopes are slightly convex. The margin is oval in outline. The apex just front of center. The exterior is sculptured by irregularly spaced, fine radial ribs. The exterior is gray-brown to olive, with white rays or a checkerboard pattern. The interior edge has a relatively dull, dark band showing white markings of the exterior, and it is not sharply set off from rest of interior, which is blue-white or yellow-white; the interior apex may be irregularly marked with brown.

From the Pribilof and Aleutian islands to southern California. Found on mid- and lower intertidal rock surfaces. Feeds on algae scraped from rocks with its radula. *N. scutum* can be distinguished from other limpets by its location in the lower intertidal zone, its flat profile and large size, and its fine sculpturing.

63   *Notoacmea persona*

Length of shell to 5 centimeters (2 inches); height about one-half length. The shell is conical. The frontal slope of the shell is straight; all others are convex. The apex is located one-fourth to one-third of the total length from the front edge. The exterior has fine, radial ribs. Exterior is brown to olive with lighter rays or patches; the border of the interior shell is dark, the intermediate area blue-white; apex is irregularly marked with brown.

From the Shumagin Islands to central California. Upper intertidal on rock surfaces. *Collisella pelta* reaches about the same size and has similar coloration, but it usually occurs in the low intertidal zone and may be marked by more noticeably irregular, radial ribs.

64   *Diodora aspera* — Keyhole Limpet

Length of shell to about 6.4 centimeters (2½ inches); height about one-third length. The shell is conical with an oval outline. The apex is closer to the front than the back edge. At the apex there is a rounded opening equal in length to about one-tenth the total shell length. The shell's exterior has coarse radial ribs; large ribs usually alternate with several finer ribs; all are crossed by concentric lines. The shell's interior has a small, flattened area circling the apical opening. The exterior is gray-white, occasionally with dark brown radiating bands; the interior is white.

From Baja California to Prince William Sound and Afognak Island. Found on rocky surfaces from the low intertidal zone to a depth of 40 meters (21.8 fathoms). Feeds by scraping algae and other materials from rocks.

65 *Puncturella cucullata* — Keyhole Limpet

Length of shell to about 2.5 centimeters (1 inch); height about three-fourths length. The shell is conical. The apex is pointed and hooked toward the front end of the shell. Immediately behind the apex is a narrow, elongate, vertical slit. Inside the shell at the apex, a small, horizontal septum covers the upper part of the slit. The shell's exterior has 13-23 major radial ribs alternating with groups of 3-6 secondary ribs. The shell edge is scalloped by the ends of the major ribs. Cream to dingy white inside and out.

From Kodiak Island to Baja California. Low intertidal and sub-tidal to at least 20 meters (10.9 fathoms); tends to be deeper in its southern range. Five other species of *Puncturella* occur in Alaskan waters.

Abalone

66 *Haliotis kamtschatkana* — Northern Abalone, Pinto Abalone

Length of shell to about 13.3 centimeters (5¼ inches). Shell is ear-shaped, low, thin and oval. Spire is low. The last whorl has 3-6 open holes near margin; older holes sealed. The exterior surface is rough, marked by irregular lumps and fine cords. Shell exterior is a mottled mixture of dull reds and greens; shell interior is iridescent.

From Cross Sound in Southeastern Alaska to Baja California. Low intertidal to about 20 meters (10.9 fathoms) in Alaskan waters; often deeper in its southern range. Occurs on rela-tively open, coasts or along major inland straits. It clings very tightly to rock surfaces when disturbed, but can move more rapidly than most gastropods when approached by a natural predator, such as the sea star *Pycnopodia helianthoides*. When reacting to the predator, the abalone lifts its shell well off the substrate and moves away at a speed of 25 centimeters (about 10 inches) or more per minute. It feeds on diatoms and algae. Its shell is often heavily encrusted by other marine organisms.

Juveniles, which are rarely seen, usually hide under rocks. This is the only species of abalone found in Alaskan waters.

Snails

67 *Margarites pupillus*

Height of shell to about 1.3 centimeters (½ inch). Shaped like a turban, approximately as broad as it is high. Has about 5 whorls, each with 5-6 smooth, fine, spiral cords and microscopic, axial, slanting threads. The aperture is round. The umbilicus has a small, narrow opening. Exterior is a dull, pink to gray; aperture is pearly pink.

From the Bering Sea to southern California. Intertidal and shallow subtidal. Usually found on rocky surfaces. A herbivore. *M. helicinus,* a smaller member of the genus (height to 8 millimeters/⅓ inch), is often found on large algae and can be distinguished from *M. pupillus* by its smooth exterior surface. A number of other species of the genus are also recorded in Alaskan waters.

68 *Calliostoma ligatum*

Height of shell to 2.5 centimeters (1 inch). The species is shaped like a turban and is approximately as broad as high. Has about 7 rounded whorls. The aperture is round. The operculum is circular and horny. The umbilicus is covered. The exterior is tan to brown with the spiral cords being slightly lighter in color; the interior is iridescent blue-green to pink.

From southern California to as far north as Southeastern Alaska. Intertidal and shallow subtidal. Eggs are laid in gelatinous ribbons.

69 *Calliostoma annulatum*

Height of shell to about 3.2 centimeters (1¼ inches); the shell is slightly less wide than high. Has 8-9 whorls. The sutures between the whorls are slightly indented. The base of the body whorl is nearly flat. Sculpture consists of spiraling rows of minute, distinct beads. Shell is golden yellow with tones of brown; the lower edge of each whorl has a spiraling violet band.

From southern California to Prince William Sound. Subtidal. This species differs from *C. ligatum* by its violet band just above the sutures and by the beaded quality of the spiral sculpture. Two additional species also occur in Alaskan waters but are less common.

70 *Lacuna carinata*

Height of shell to about 1.3 centimeters (½ inch) — slightly less than its width. The shell has 3-5 fragile, smooth whorls. The aperture is wide with a thin outer lip. Umbilicus is conspicuous, white, slender and curving. The shell is covered with a yellow-brown periostracum. The color pattern is variable, often with spiral bands of brown and yellow or white.

From the Bering Sea to mid-California. Intertidal and shallow subtidal. Often found on kelp. Several species of *Lacuna* are found in Alaskan waters. *L. variegata* is usually found on eelgrass and has a shell that measures about 6 millimeters (¼ inch) high. *L. vincta* is distinguished from *L. carinata* by its taller spire and narrower, tan umbilical groove.

71 *Littorina sitkana* — Periwinkle

Height of shell to about 1.9 centimeters (¾ inch). The shell is rotund, almost as wide as high. Has no umbilicus. The aperture is about one-half shell height. Strong, spiral cords mark the body whorl. The operculum is horny and thin. The shell is usually solid gray to brown and may have dull white spiral bands or other color variations; the operculum is brown.

From the Bering Sea and Aleutian Islands to Puget Sound. Mid to upper intertidal. May be extremely common on rocky shores. Feeds by scraping minute organisms from rocks with a ribbonlike radula.

72 *Littorina scutulata* — Periwinkle

Height of shell to about 1.9 centimeters (¾ inch). The shell is slender, width about two-thirds of height. Has no umbilicus. The operculum is horny. The shell may be a uniform shade of light to dark brown or purple and may be marked with irregular white checkerboarding; the operculum is brown.

From Baja California to Southeastern Alaska. Intertidal and found on rocky surfaces. Not as abundant as *L. sitkana* from which it may be distinguished by its taller spire, more slender appearance, and lack of spiral cords or white spiral banding. Feeds by scraping organic material from rocks.

73　*Epitonium greenlandicum* — Wentletrap

Height of shell to about 3.8 centimeters (1½ inches); greatest width about one-third its height; height of aperture is less than one-fourth total shell height. The spire is tall with 8-9 whorls, each having about 9 broad, flattened, axial ribs with underlying spiral cords; the body whorl has 6 ribs. The aperture is round. Has no canal. The operculum is dark and fits the aperture snugly. Ribs are pure white; the remaining exterior is gray-white to purple-white; interior, white.

From British Columbia to the Bering Sea. Subtidal to about 240 meters (131 fathoms). Uncommon. Four other species of *Epitonium* are found in Alaskan waters.

74　*Trichotropis cancellata*

Height of shell to about 2.5 centimeters (1 inch). The spire is tall and usually eroded. The aperture is large, round and equal to about one-third total shell height. The canal is short. The operculum is flexible and fits snugly into the aperture. The shell has 6-7 whorls, is thin and sculptured with axial cords; strong spiral cords produce a crosshatch pattern. Exterior of shell is yellow-white; the periostracum is light tan with rows of long, bristlelike projections along the spiral cords; the interior of shell is white or tinged with yellow.

From the Bering Sea to Oregon. Shallow subtidal. Inhabits areas with currents and often perches on slight prominences, such as worm tubes or boulders. It is a filter feeder that collects food particles in mucus and transports them to the mouth by the movement of cilia. Individuals to about 2.4 centimeters (1 inch) in height and 1 year of age are males; they then transform into females. Spawning occurs in the spring. Individual egg capsules are disk shaped. Four additional species of *Trichotropis* are recorded in Alaska.

75　*Natica clausa* — Moon Snail

Height of shell to about 5.7 centimeters (2¼ inches); width slightly less than height. Spherical. Has about 5 whorls with the body whorl making up most of shell; the whorls are slightly flattened below the suture. The aperture is almost semicircular. Has no canal. The umbilicus is completely covered. The operculum is calcareous, shiny, nearly as thick as the shell itself, and contoured to fit the aperture snugly. The periostracum is thin and flakes off easily. The exterior is tan, often lighter at the base of the shell; the interior is white with irregular brown markings.

From the Arctic Ocean and Aleutian Islands to California. Intertidal to as deep as 1800 meters (984 fathoms). Often buried in sand. Feeds on clams by boring a small, conical hole in one valve. Eggs are deposited in a collarlike case of sand grains cemented together by a mucus secretion.

76 *Lunatia lewisii* — Moon Snail

Height of shell to about 13 centimeters (5 inches); width slightly less than height. Spherical. Of the 4-6 whorls, the body whorl makes up most of the shell; whorls are wrinkled and somewhat flattened just below suture; below the wrinkled area, a broad, shallow, spiraling indentation is evident. The aperture is nearly semicircular. The umbilicus is open, rounded and deep. The periostracum is thin. The operculum is horny and shaped to fit the aperture snugly. The shell's exterior is light yellow-tan; interior is mottled white and brown.

From southern Southeastern Alaska to Baja California. Intertidal to about 45 meters (24.6 fathoms). Found on sand or fine gravel, where it burrows and feeds on clams, leaving the shells with a conical, bored hole in one valve. When this snail is undisturbed, its mantle extends up over the shell, nearly covering it. Eggs are deposited in a collarlike case of cemented sand grains. Another species, *L. pallida*, is found from the Arctic to California, grows to only 4.4 centimeters (1¾ inches), and has an umbilicus that is opened slightly.

77 *Fusitriton oregonensis* — Hairy Triton

Height of shell to about 13 centimeters (5 inches). Has about 6 whorls, each with 16-18 low, rounded axial ribs; many-spiraled cords cross the ribs. The aperture is wide and narrows to an open canal. The shell is very fragile and covered by a heavy, brown periostracum with spirally arranged bristles; the shell's exterior is tan, interior is white; the horny operculum is brown.

From the Pribilof and Aleutian islands to southern California. Low intertidal to deep water. The spire is usually eroded. The periostracum is often partially or totally worn off, and, if so, the shell is likely to be encrusted with coralline algae or any of numerous invertebrates. The brachiopod *Terebratulina unguicula* often attaches itself near the apex, and a low, slipper shell, *Crepidula* sp., may be found on the operculum. The snail is carnivorous, sometimes feeding by scavenging or boring holes in the tests of sea urchins. In the spring and early summer large groups gather to spawn. Egg cases, shaped like kernels of corn, are attached in compact spirals to sloping or vertical rock surfaces. The photo of *Fusitriton oregonensis* on page 21 shows egg cases.

78   *Nucella lamellosa* — Dogwinkle

Height of shell to about 8.2 centimeters (3¼ inches). The canal is short and the operculum horny. The spire may be short or tall; spiral cords are usually evident and on the upper whorls may be the only sculpturing. The axial ribs may be well developed or barely evident; the ribs of specimens found in protected waters may be more elaborate and distinct than those in exposed waters. May be white, gray, orange, purple or spirally banded.

From the Bering Strait to southern California. Found primarily in low intertidal and shallow subtidal zones. Prefers a rocky surface. This is a carnivorous snail that often preys on barnacles. In the spring, large numbers gather to spawn. Egg capsules, resembling yellow, stalked oats in size and shape, are deposited in dense patches. Three other species of *Nucella* are found in Alaskan waters, none of which has prominent axial ribs. *N. canaliculata* has a high spire and is often color banded. It has deep grooves between its prominent spiral cords. *N. lima* has fine spiral cords, is rarely color banded and usually is white to orange-brown. *N. emarginata* has alternating large and small spiral cords that are often scaled or noduled. It may have narrow color banding.

79   *Ceratostoma foliatum* — Leafy Hornmouth

Height of shell to about 8.2 centimeters (3¼ inches). The shell has about 6 whorls, each with 3 prominent, shelflike, axial projections forming a broken ridge from the apex to the lower edge of the shell; projections spiral in a direction opposite to that of the shell's growth; the last projection on the body whorl terminates in a closed, flattened canal. Spiral cords, widely spaced at the upper portion of the whorl, form scallops with the edges of the projections. The aperture is oval and has a large tooth at the lower edge next to the last projection. The operculum is horny. The shell's exterior is often a dark gray-brown, fading to white along the edge of the last projection; occasionally, it is white with wide, dark brown bands; the interior is white.

From southern California to Southeastern Alaska. Found in low intertidal zones to about 65 meters (35.5 fathoms). Found on rocks. This snail is often heavily encrusted with bryozoans and tube worms. Its spire is usually eroded. *C. foliatum* is carnivorous and feeds on barnacles. Egg cases are yellow.

80 *Boreotrophon stuarti*

Height of shell to about 5 centimeters (2 inches); width about one-half height. Has about 6 sharply shouldered whorls. The canal is long, slender and curving. The sculpture has weak spiral cords, about 5 on the body whorl, and distinctive wing-like axial lamellae, 9-11 per whorl. The lamellae are thin, delicate, wide, and usually project upward above the upper edge of the whorl. Pure white to yellow-white and may have a greenish appearance.

From the Shumagin Islands to southern California. Low intertidal to at least 24 meters (13.1 fathoms). About 15 species of *Boreotrophon* have been recorded in Alaskan waters. Members of the group generally have a long, slender canal and winglike lamellae. Some specimens appear to be intermediate between 2 described species, making their identification difficult.

81 *Amphissa columbiana*

Height of shell to about 2.5 centimeters (1 inch); and spindle-shaped. The aperture is narrow, and the canal short; outer lip of aperture is thick, straight in upper two-thirds, then rounded at the bottom. With about 6 whorls. The exterior is sculptured by numerous weak, axial ribs, except for lower part of last whorl, which is without axial ribs but has fine, spiral ribs. The periostracum is thin and yellow; operculum horny; exterior of shell is usually a dull pink-brown or yellow-brown, often irregularly mottled.

From southern California to Prince William Sound. Intertidal and shallow subtidal zones. *A. columbiana* is carnivorous and often scavenges; many individuals may collect on one dead organism.

82   *Buccinum plectrum*

Height of shell to 7.6 centimeters (3 inches); width about one-half height. The shell is moderately heavy and with up to 7 whorls. The spire is high and sharp. The aperture is broad, and about one-third total shell height; lip of aperture is S-curved, thickened into a rim, and flared. The external sculpture has low, curving axial ribs, which on the body whorl, resemble the S-curve of the aperture; with many minute, incised, spiraling lines. The operculum is smaller than the aperture and horny. The shell exterior is chalky white and covered by a thin, orange-brown periostracum; interior is white and glazed.

From the Arctic Ocean to Puget Sound. Subtidal to about 90 meters (49.2 fathoms). *B. glaciale*, another subtidal species, has minimal axial sculpturing and a few strong, spiral cords that alternate with groups of incised, spiral lines. More than 40 species of *Buccinum* have been recorded in Alaskan waters, most of them in the Arctic Ocean and the Bering Sea. When the group is thoroughly studied many of these may prove to be variants rather than true species.

83   *Volutharpa ampullacea*

Height of shell to 3.8 centimeters (1½ inches); width three-fourths height. The shell is fragile and globose. The spire is short, leaving most of shell to consist of the body whorl. Aperture large, about two-thirds shell height; aperture lip flares in adults; the canal is short and operculum small and round (may be absent). Exterior is covered with a gray-brown, velvety periostracum; aperture of young specimens is brown; large individuals, yellow-green to orange; interior, glassy.

From the Bering Sea to Vancouver Island, British Columbia. Shallow subtidal to deep water. Another species, *V. perryi,* is recorded in the Bering Sea.

84   *Colus halli*

Height of shell to about 5 centimeters (2 inches); width less than one-half height. The shell is slender with 5-6 whorls. The aperture is oval and the canal short. Operculum is horny. The shell exterior is smooth without sculpturing, except for microscopic, incised, spiral lines. Exterior is chalky white, covered by a thin, smooth periostracum that is yellow-brown to dark brown; interior shell is white.

From the Bering Sea to southern California. Subtidal and usually found on sandy bottoms. A scavenger; often taken in baited pots. About 30 species of *Colus* have been recorded in Alaskan waters, but some of these may be variants and not true species.

85 *Neptunea lirata*

Height of shell to about 13 centimeters (5 inches); width three-fourths height. The shell is fairly heavy, with about 6 whorls; exterior shell has coarse, spiral cords (about 8-12 on the body whorl) alternating with several finer cords; usually two spiral cords are visible on each whorl of the spire. The aperture is oval, elongate and ends with a wide, straight canal. The operculum is horny and considerably smaller than the aperture. Shell exterior is tan to gray; shell interior is light at aperture, darker within.

From the Bering Sea to California. In Alaska, intertidal to about 90 meters (49.2 fathoms), much deeper in southern range. Spawns in late winter or early spring, depositing columns of overlapping, scalelike egg capsules, each with many eggs inside. Empty shells are usually inhabited by large hermit crabs. *N. pribiloffensis* is similar to *N. lirata* but has an aperture lip that flares more noticeably, weaker primary cords, and secondary cording that is more pronounced and visible on all older whorls. *N. pribiloffensis* is strictly subtidal and reaches greater depths than *N. lirata*. Some specimens appear to be intermediate between the two species. In the Bering Sea, species of *Neptunea* are harvested by the Japanese for food.

86 *Searlesia dira*

Height of shell to about 3.8 centimeters (1½ inches); width about one-half height. The shell is spindle-shaped with about 5 rounded whorls, weak, rounded axial ribs in the spire, and conspicuous spiral threads overall. The aperture is oval and its interior edge reflects exterior sculpturing. The canal is short and slightly twisted to the left. The operculum is horny. Shell exterior is dark gray-brown; interior, brown to dull purple.

From central California, to Prince William Sound. Low intertidal and subtidal, often found on rocky surfaces. Carnivorous; at least in part a scavenger that feeds on fish carcasses and other dead animal material.

Cephalaspidean

87 *Gastropteron pacificum*

Length to about 2.5 centimeters (1 inch). The small, coiled, calcareous shell is contained within a sacklike body. Has two, large, fleshy, winglike fins, one on each side. The body is yellow with red flecks.

From the Gulf of California to Southeastern Alaska. Occurs from about 2-426 meters (1-233 fathoms). Although it may swim with a flapping motion in quiet waters, the species usually crawls on the bottom. An opisthobranch. It is not common. *Limacina helicina,* another swimming snail occurring in Alaskan waters, has an external shell about 0.2 centimeters ($\frac{1}{12}$ inch) in length and two winglike, lateral fins. *L. helicina* serves as food for salmon and whales in northern waters.

Notaspidean

88 *Berthella californica*

Length to about 5 centimeters (2 inches). The body is oval, arched and soft. The mantle has a wavy edge extending beyond the sides of foot and a deep, wide notch at the anterior edge. Blunt, cylindrical rhinophores project through the anterior mantle notch. An external gill-plume on the right side is concealed between the edge of the mantle and the foot. The mantle covers a thin, oblong, internal, shell that has a small, spiral nucleus and a thin periostracum. The mantle is translucent white to cream and flecked with opaque white.

From southern California to the Aleutian Islands. Subtidal; intertidal in southern range. May feed on ascidians and sponges. Resembles the nudibranchs but differs in having an internal shell.

Nudibranchs

89 *Triopha catalinae*

Length to about 15.2 centimeters (6 inches); the body is elongate, and rounded at its anterior end, bluntly pointed at posterior end. The dorsal surface is granular with irregularly distributed tubercles. Rhinophores retract into prominent sheaths. Five plumelike, branching, retractile external gills lie in a circle on the dorsal surface. White with orange on tips of gills, rhinophores, tubercles, and edge of rhinophore sheaths.

From the Aleutian Islands to southern California. Shallow subtidal to 18 meters (9.8 fathoms) in Alaska. Occurs intertidally in southern range. Feeds on bryozoans. Lays its eggs in the spring or summer in white, coiled ribbons.

90 *Cadlina luteomarginata*

Length usually to about 3.8 centimeters (1½ inches), occasionally to 6.4 centimeters (2½ inches). The body is elongate and oval. The dorsal surface is covered with small tubercles. The mantle covers the head and most of the foot. Rhinophores are small, conical, retractile and have 16-18 leaves. Six plumelike, retractile, external gills lie in a circle on the posterior dorsal surface. White or very pale yellow, except for the tips of the tubercles, gills, rhinophores, and the edge of mantle, which are lemon yellow.

From Baja California, to at least Prince William Sound. Shallow subtidal to about 18 meters (9.8 fathoms). Usually found on bedrock. Feeds on sponges.

91 *Diaulula sandiegensis*

Length to about 8.2 centimeters (3¼ inches). The dorsal surface is velvety, textured by minute tubercles. Mantle completely covers head; tip of foot shows from under the mantle at posterior end. Rhinophores are conical, each with 20-30 leaves, retractile into conspicuous, flaring sheaths. Six plumelike, retractile external gills lie in a circle on the dorsal surface. White to pale gray or brown, with dark brown or black rings or blotches scattered on the dorsal surface.

From the Aleutian Islands to Baja California. Subtidal in Alaska; intertidally in southern range. Feeds on sponges.

92   *Lamellidoris fusca*

Length to about 3.8 centimeters (1½ inches). The dorsal surface is covered with wartlike tubercles. The foot extends beyond the mantle at posterior end. Rhinophores retract into low sheaths. Has 16-32 (or more) simple, small, somewhat contractable, external gills on the posterior, dorsal surface. White to rust with an irregular pattern of brown markings which are often concentrated in 2 or 3 longitudinal bands on the dorsal surface; rhinophores, tan; gills, brown.

From Baja California, to at least Southeastern Alaska. Low intertidal and shallow subtidal. Congregates in dense groups, usually on barnacles, on which they feed.

93   *Dendronotus rufus*

Length to about 28 centimeters (11 inches). The body is long and slender. Has 5 pairs of branched processes at anterior edge. Each of 2 rhinophores is surrounded by a sheath with 5 branched processes; with 7 or 8 pairs of branching processes distributed along the body's dorsal surface. Usually white with magenta on tips of all body appendages; occasionally, specimens have a mid-dorsal magenta stripe; a magenta line trims the edge of the foot.

From Southeastern Alaska to Puget Sound. Shallow subtidal and found on wharves, pilings and rocky surfaces. Feeds on scyphistomae, the sedentary polyp stage of the large, scyphozoan jellyfishes, and to a lesser extent on bryozoans. No predators on *D. rufus* are known, but it does react to the sea stars *Pycnopodia helianthoides* and *Crossaster papposus* with vigorous swimming. Life span is one year; spawns January to March, often gathering in groups to deposit eggs in large patches on rocks or pilings. Dies after spawning.

94   *Dendronotus iris*

Length to about 20.3 centimeters (8 inches). The body is slender with rounded anterior and tapered posterior ends. The anterior edge has a series of unbranched and branched processes. Each of 2 rhinophores, which are large, forward slanting and retractile, is surrounded by 5-6 similar branching processes. The dorsal surface has 5-6 additional pairs of branching processes. The coloration is variable: may be gray-white to dark brown with dark purple or yellow on the tips of body appendages; or the species may be orange-red with metallic orange or opaque white tips; coloration is often between these two extremes.

From Unalaska to Baja California. Shallow subtidal to at least 200 meters (109.4 fathoms). Usually found on mud or sandy bottoms. Feeds on burrowing anemones, eating their tentacles. Probably spawns in late winter or early spring. The larvae are planktonic, and *D. iris* reaches maturity in as little as 3-4 months. Preyed upon by sea stars and possibly by anemones and fish. Swims readily if disturbed and most violently in the presence of the sea star *Pycnopodia helianthoides*. The specimen shown on page 25 is swimming in midwater.

95 *Tritonia festiva*

Length to about 8.2 centimeters (3¼ inches). The body is tapered. The foot extends beyond the sides of the mantle. The dorsal surface is smooth or slightly rough. The anterior margin has 8-12 slender, tapering processes. Rhinophores at the mantle's edge are stout and retract into large, flaring sheaths. The edge of the mantle thickens into a ridge with 11-15 plumelike external gills on each side. Cream to yellow, orange or yellow-brown; irregular opaque white lines outline the foot, the edge of the rhinophore sheaths and the edge of the mantle; the foot is transparent and thin.

From Kenai Peninsula to Baja California. Subtidal to at least 25 meters (13.7 fathoms). *T. festiva* will swim if disturbed.

96 *Tochuina tetraquetra*

Length to 30.5 centimeters (12 inches) or more — usually about 15.2 centimeters (6 inches) long. The body is stout, narrowing at posterior to a rounded tail; it is highest near mid-body and tapers to both ends. The dorsal surface is covered with large and small tubercles. The edge of the mantle is wavy, with an irregular series of low, plumelike external gills. Rhinophores retract into high, thick-walled sheaths. The foot is broad and smooth and nearly as wide as the mantle. Yellow-orange; external gills are white; the tubercles are tipped with white.

From Unalaska Island to southern California. Shallow subtidal to about 27 meters (14.8 fathoms). Found on shell and gravel or rock surfaces. Spawns in the spring. Feeds on the soft coral

Gersemia and perhaps on the sea pen, *Ptilosarcus.* The largest of the Pacific Coast nudibranchs.

97 *Melibe leonina*

Length to about 17.8 centimeters (7 inches). The body is slender and smooth and tapers gradually from the head to tip of its rounded tail. The head expands into an elliptical hood and is separated from the body by a narrow neck. Hood margin has 2 series of slender projections. Rhinophores are widely separated, located on dorsal surface of hood; 5-6 pairs of large, flat cerata are located on the dorsal body surface. Colorless and translucent; the opaque-yellow, branching digestive gland is visible in body and cerata.

From Kodiak Island and Prince William Sound to Baja California. Shallow subtidal to about 18 meters (9.8 fathoms). Usually located on kelp or eelgrass. May be abundant locally. Its food is small crustaceans, such as amphipods and copepods, and other plankton. It feeds by sweeping its fringed hood through the water, closing the hood at the end of each stroke. Does this repeatedly if not disturbed, each sweep taking about a minute. Swims weakly and will occasionally be seen in midwater or near the surface with the foot up and the body flexing alternately to the right and left.

98 *Armina californica*

Length to 5 centimeters (2 inches). The body is high in front and slopes to a pointed tail. The mantle edge has a rounded notch in front. Rhinophores located in the notch are short, blunt, close together and retractile. External gills lie hidden under each side of the mantle. The foot is broad, flat, smooth. The dorsal surface is light pink-brown to brown or black with white, wavy, longitudinal ridges along the length of the mantle; the foot and mantle are edged with white.

From Southeastern Alaska to Panama. Shallow subtidal to 80 meters (43.7 fathoms) or more. Found on sand. Burrows, leaving only the tips of the rhinophores visible. Eggs are deposited in light pink-brown, convoluted ribbons. Feeds on anemones, including *Metridium,* and on sea pens.

99 *Dirona albolineata*

Length to 18 centimeters (7½ inches). The body is broad and

smooth and tapers from a blunt, rounded head to a short, pointed tail. The head has a broad, extended covering, or veil. Rhinophores without sheaths point forward. Dorsal cerata are lance-shaped and smooth; cerata occur both ahead and behind the rhinophores. Translucent gray with narrow bands of opaque white on the edges of the veil, dorsal cerata and tail.

From Southeastern Alaska to southern California. Shallow subtidal to about 27 meters (14.7 fathoms). Found on a variety of surfaces. Feeds on small snails, ascidians and bryozoans.

100 *Dirona aurantia*

Length to 15.2 centimeters (6 inches). The body is broad at its anterior end, tapering to a pointed tail. Rhinophores without sheaths are present. Dorsal cerata are lance-shaped and smooth with cerata occurring both ahead and behind rhinophores. Bright to very pale translucent orange with a few white granular spots and opaque white markings on tips and margins of cerata.

From Norton Sound to Puget Sound. Shallow subtidal to about 55 meters (30 fathoms); on rock, mud, or sand-silt substrate. Bering Sea and Norton Sound specimens tend to have paler coloration than specimens from more southerly waters.

101 *Coryphella fusca*

Length to about 12 centimeters (4¾ inches). The body is slender. Anterior tentacles are smooth, long and tapering. Rhinophores are wrinkled and tapering. Numerous slender, pointed cerata are arranged in groups in transverse rows. The body is translucent white; cerata are tipped with opaque white; a dark, internal line, part of the digestive gland, is visible for the length of each ceras.

From Prince William Sound to Oregon. Subtidal to about 30 meters (16.4 fathoms). Usually found on soft, mud-silt substrate, but also on rock surfaces. Spawns in late winter or early spring.

102 *Hermissenda crassicornis*

Length to 8.2 centimeters (3¼ inches). The slender body tapers from the anterior end to a long tail. The tentacles are long and tapering. Rhinophores stand nearly erect and are about two-thirds as long as anterior tentacles. Cerata in 5-6 groups, lance-shaped, curving gently to pointed tips. Color pattern complex and variable; body, translucent gray; mid-dorsal surface with light blue and orange to yellow longitudinal bands; cerata, tipped with white, banded with yellow and sometimes with a longitudinal blue-white line; an internal dark line, part of the digestive gland, is visible for the length of each ceras.

From Southeastern Alaska to Baja California. Low intertidal to at least 30 meters (16.4 fathoms); on various substrates—mud, rock, wood debris and pilings. Diet varied; scavenges or eats hydroids, jellyfish that have settled to the bottom, ascidians, and molluscs. Nematocysts, or stinging capsules, of hydroids and jellyfish may be stored in tips of cerata, perhaps as a means of protection. Cerata are readily cast off, and can be regenerated. Eggs are deposited in pale-pink coiled ribbons.

103 *Aeolidia papillosa*

Length to 10 centimeters (4 inches). The body tapers from a broad head to a pointed tail. Anterior tentacles taper and are slightly shorter than the rhinophores. Rhinophores are tapered and smooth. Cerata are flattened, lance-shaped and tightly grouped; arranged in 24 transverse rows, the first of which is ahead of the rhinophores. The body is white to drab gray; rhinophores darker; body, rhinophores and cerata are flecked with brown to gray; with a large triangular area of white on the head in front of the rhinophores.

From central California to at least Southeastern Alaska. Shallow subtidal to about 365 meters (200 fathoms). Feeds on such anemones as *Stomphia, Metridium* and *Tealia.*

Pulmonate

104 *Siphonaria thersites*

Shell length to about 1.3 centimeters (½ inch). The shell is conical, like that of a limpet; apex of shell forward of center and to one side; no operculum present in adults; a groove that accommodates the siphon makes the right edge of shell wavy; horseshoe-shaped muscle scar on interior of shell is open on the right side. The exterior shell is dark brown or black, with fine concentric lines and a few radial ribs, often eroded and exposing a white inner shell layer; interior of shell, dark and shiny.

From Aleutian Islands to Puget Sound. Intertidal on rock surfaces. This pulmonate can be distinguished from limpets by the relatively large mass of soft tissue and by the muscle scar on the shell interior. (Limpets also have a horseshoe-shaped scar, but it is open at the front end of the shell rather than at the right side.)

Class Bivalvia — Clams, Cockles, Mussels, Scallops and Their Allies

Bivalves, as their name indicates, have a shell made up of two pieces, or valves. These are joined by a ligament and a hinge. The valves are calcareous and are secreted by the mantle. Each valve has three layers — a lustrous, inner nacreous layer, the adjacent chalky layer, and an outer, thin layer of organic material called the periostracum. The last of these is often darker than the underlying material, may be as hard as varnish, or may be a fibrous coating that peels off readily. These two valves may be similar or different in size and shape, but they always correspond to the right and the left sides of the animal even though some bivalves, such as scallops and jingles, may look as if their valves are top and bottom.

Most bivalves are adapted for burrowing or boring, or for living permanently or semi-permanently attached to a surface. They do not have well-developed heads and their sensory receptors are usually minimal. Burrowing species, such as cockles and clams, have a large, extendable foot for digging into the substrate. Attached bivalves have only a rudimentary foot, and may produce a cement or byssal threads of organic material to better fasten themselves to hard surfaces.

Inside a bivalve's shell, strong adductor muscles attached to the valves may contract or relax to close the shell or allow the shell to open so the animal can feed and respire. In the empty shell, the places where the adductor muscles were attached appear as shiny scars. The relative sizes and shapes of the scars are often important in determining species.

In general, bivalves are ciliary feeders. Water is drawn into the animal, often through an incurrent siphon, and passes the ctenidia, a structure that functions in respiration. As respiration is taking place, microscopic particles of food are trapped in mucus and transported by ciliary action to the animal's mouth. Water that has passed over the ctenidia then moves out of the animal, usually via a distinct excurrent siphon.

Most bivalves have separate sexes, although some are hermaphroditic. Fertilization is usually external and the larvae that develop from the fertilized eggs swim freely before they settle to the sea floor and metamorphose to the adult form.

Measurements given for bivalves include shell height and length. Height is the distance in one plane from the beak of the shell (the peaked area near the hinge and the focus of the concentric growth) to the opposite margin. Length is a front-to-back distance that intersects at a 90-degree angle the line used to measure height.

Shipworm

105 *Bankia setacea*

Valves of shell are very small, rough and specialized for boring; they are borne at anterior end of a long, wormlike body; height equal to about one-fortieth the animal's total length; entire animal is as long as 91 centimeters (3 feet).

From the Bering Sea to Baja California. Found in drifting logs, wooden boat hulls, or wood debris exposed to the marine environment. As larvae, shipworms settle on wood and begin boring into it. Generally following the grain of the wood, they create long burrows as much as 1.9 centimeters (¾ inch) in diameter and lined with a white calcareous casing secreted by the shipworm's mantle. Some of the cellulose eroded by the boring activity is apparently digested as food, but much of it passes out of the animal undigested and is carried out of the burrow by water currents. The shipworm also feeds on microscopic organisms it filters from water circulating through it. The animal causes damage to wood left in salt water, but can be regarded as a key biological factor in the breakdown and disintegration of wood debris that enters the sea. This is the only species of shipworm common in the northeastern Pacific Ocean. It is sometimes erroneously called *Teredo*, a genus name more properly applied to a group of shipworms seldom found north of California. In the photo on page 28, the shipworms are largely hidden in the log; only their siphons and accumulated waste material are visible.

Mussels

106   *Mytilus edulis* — Blue Mussel

Length of shell to about 9 centimeters (3½ inches); height about one-half length. Beak is located at anterior tip of shell. Hinge has 4-6 teeth. Without radiating ribs, but with coarse, concentric growth lines. Usually covered with a blue-black, varnishlike periostracum; shell beneath periostracum, chalky purple; occasional individuals may have a periostracum that is yellow-brown; interior of shell is slightly pearly and blue-white.

Circumpolar; from the Arctic Ocean to Baja California. Usually intertidal, where it forms dense patches or beds covering bedrock and rubble surfaces, but often subtidal in northern areas such as Norton Sound; also occurs on undersides of floats, on mooring lines, and on other floating objects. Attaches to substrate by byssal threads. An important food for sea gulls, crows, surf scoters, sea and river otters, fishes such as the wolf eel, and sea stars such as *Evasterias troschelii.* Harvested for human consumption in Europe, but in Alaskan waters may be highly poisonous to humans due to strong concentrations of a toxin obtained from one of the planktonic organisms on which it feeds. *M. californianus* is a similar species but it reaches 25.4 centimeters (10 inches) in length, and occurs only on more-exposed shores from the Aleutian Islands to California.

107   *Musculus niger*

Length of shell to about 8.2 centimeters (3¼ inches); height about one-half length. Beak is located close to anterior end of shell. The hinge has fine teeth. The shell has 3 distinct areas: a smooth, central area; a large, posterior end; and a smaller, anterior end; both ends have well-developed radial ribs. Exterior shell is nearly black; interior may be tinged with pink.

From the Arctic Ocean to Puget Sound. Subtidal to about 120 meters (65.6 fathoms). This mussel may encase itself in a cocoon of byssal threads in which the young are sheltered. Three similar species occur in Alaska. *M. discors* has an inflated shell, weak radial ribs (more evident on the anterior than posterior end), and is dark, olive brown. *M. olivaceus* has a small shell with a length to about 1 centimeter (about

½ inch) and a lustrous, light-olive periostracum. *M. vernicosus* is common along the outer coast of Southeastern Alaska and in the Kodiak Island area. It is found in great numbers on large algae.

108 *Modiolus modiolus* — Northern Horse Mussel

Length of shell commonly to about 15.2 centimeters (6 inches); height about one-half length. Anterior end of shell extends a short distance beyond beak. Hinge is without teeth. Shell is heavy, with a thin, yellow-brown periostracum or a rather thick, purple-black, varnishlike periostracum that flakes off when the shell is dried. Long, smooth hairs are a part of the periostracum; shells of large specimens are a chalky, lavender-white beneath the periostracum.

From southern California to the Pribilof Islands. Subtidal and often found in dense patches on sand or gravel at 10-15 meters (5-8 fathoms). One of the largest subtidal mussels.

Scallops

109 *Chlamys rubida*

Length of shell to about 7 centimeters (2¾ inches). Has a rounded outline and is moderately flattened. "Ears" are distinctly unequal in size. Upper (left) valve has numerous primary radial ribs, each bearing nearly microscopic spines alternating with much smaller ribs that also bear fine spines; the lower (right) valve is flat, usually lighter in color, and with a few smooth, rounded, and sometimes paired ribs. Shell color is variable: pink, lavender, yellow, yellow-orange, or blends; mantle, which is visible at edge of live, gaping shell, bears sensory tentacles and numerous tiny eyes.

From southern California, to Southeastern Alaska. Subtidal. Taken by dredge down to 1,600 meters (874 fathoms). Usually found at 10-25 meters (5-14 fathoms) on sand, gravel, boulders, or bedrock; may become attached to a hard substrate by byssal threads. Characteristically it rests with right valve on substrate; upper valve is frequently encrusted with sponge or other organisms. It is capable of swimming several feet off bottom by clapping valves together and expelling water through openings on either side of the hinge.

110 *Chlamys hastata hericia*

Length of shell to about 8.2 centimeters (3¼ inches). Upper left valve with about 10 primary ribs, alternating with series of smaller ribs that include a single, central rib that is only slightly smaller than the primary ribs. Lower (right) valve has about 20 primary ribs separated from each other by numerous, smaller ribs. All ribs on both valves have close-set, scalelike spines. Color is variable: pink, white, rose-brown and light yellow or a combination of these several colors.

From southern California to the Aleutian Islands. Shallow subtidal to about 37 meters (20 fathoms). Less common in Alaskan waters than in its southern range. It may be distinguished from *C. rubida,* with which it occurs, by the large spines on the ribs. The upper valve is often encrusted with sponge. Like other species of *Chlamys,* this scallop is capable of swimming and bears sensory tentacles and eyes around the edge of the mantle.

111 *Pecten caurinus* —Weathervane Scallop

Length of shell to about 21 centimeters (8¼ inches). Circular in outline. Ears are nearly equal in length. Valves are only slightly convex. Upper (left) valve is red-brown to yellow-brown, with about 20 low, rounded ribs; lower valve is a lighter color or white with an approximately equal number of broad, flat-topped ribs. Mantle, visible at shell margin, has sensory tentacles and eyes.

From the Bering Sea and Aleutian Islands to central California. Occasionally found in shallow subtidal waters but usually 10 meters (5.5 fathoms) or deeper. Often located on sand or muddy sand and resting in a slight depression. Although capable of swimming, it does not do so as readily as the smaller *Chlamys.* This scallop has supported a limited commercial fishery in Alaska.

112 *Hinnites multirugosus* — Purple-Hinged Rock Scallop

Length of shell to about 20.3 centimeters (8 inches). Outline of shell may be nearly circular or irregular and dictated by environmental conditions. Young individuals resemble *Chlamys;* older specimens have heavy, massive shells. Exterior of shell of mature specimens have primary and secondary radiating ribs, both sculptured with scalelike spines that are directed toward the edge of the shell (often too eroded and encrusted to show original sculpturing); interior of shell is white with purple at the hinge area. Mantle has about 60 eyes.

From Baja California to Southeastern Alaska. Shallow subtidal to about 60 meters (33 fathoms). Most frequently found in areas of moderate current or wave surge. Until shell reaches a diameter of 2.5-5 centimeters (1-2 inches), the animal is free-swimming, but then it usually becomes permanently cemented by the lower valve to a rock surface. Occasionally, large individuals may be found free on gravel or rubble bottoms. The shell is usually heavily encrusted with sponge, bryozoans, algae or virtually anything that grows on surrounding rock surfaces. The scallop, therefore, is often well concealed and difficult to distinguish from its surroundings when closed. The shell is often heavily bored by the yellow sponge *Cliona celata.*

Jingle

113 *Pododesmus cepio*

Diameter of valve to about 10 centimeters (4 inches). Valves are flattened, nearly circular in outline, and often deformed by environmental conditions; lower (right) valve has a large, roughly circular, opening through which a massive byssus extends to attach the animal to the substrate. Hinge is without teeth. Exterior of valves are yellow to light green with irregular, coarse, radiating ribs; interior surface is relatively smooth, green and pearly.

From the Pribilof and Aleutian islands to Baja California. Low tide mark to about 70 meters (38 fathoms) on hard surfaces. Usually attached flat against substrate but sometimes has the free edge raised. Often heavily encrusted.

Cockles

114 *Clinocardium nuttallii*

Length of shell to about 12 centimeters (4¾ inches); about as high as long. The shell is heavy, rather inflated, somewhat triangular and usually has 33-37 coarse, radial ribs roughened by blunt spines. Concentric growth rings are evident on large specimens. Young shells have a calico pattern of brown, dull red, or yellow on a lighter background; older shells are gray or yellow-brown. The periostracum is thin and not readily apparent.

From the Bering Sea to southern California. Intertidal and shallow subtidal. May be found lying on the surface, but is usually buried to a shallow depth in sand or fine gravel. Preyed upon by such sea stars as *Pycnopodia helianthoides* or *Evasterias troschelii*. Sometimes escapes predators by using its long, muscular foot to throw itself over the bottom in cartwheel fashion. Can live up to 7 years. Two smaller, less common species of *Clinocardium* occur in Alaskan waters. *C. fucanum* has a greater number of radiating ribs (45-50), and its ribs are low, rounded and relatively smooth. *C. ciliatum* has a conspicuous periostracum that includes hairlike projections atop the ribs.

115 *Serripes groenlandicus* — Greenland Cockle

Length of shell to about 10 centimeters (4 inches). The shell is thin but strong, oval to nearly round and inflated. Weak radial ribs are visible at the anterior and posterior ends of the shell. Concentric growth rings increase in prominence toward edge. Exterior of shell has fine, tan, wavering lines over a yellow to gray-green background; color patterns are more prominent on shells of young specimens.

From the Arctic Ocean to Puget Sound. Found in shallow subtidal zone down to about 120 meters (66 fathoms). Empty shells, particularly those of small specimens, are often washed ashore.

Clams

116 *Macoma inquinata*

Length of shell to about 5.7 centimeters (2¼ inches). Oval in shape. Anterior edge rounded; posterior edge tapered and wedge-shaped. Exterior of shell gray-white, with fine concentric lines; the olive-drab periostracum is evident at edge of shell; interior, white and smooth.

From the Bering Sea to southern California. Intertidal to deep water. Found in mud. At least a dozen species of *Macoma* occur in Alaskan waters. All have smooth shells, hinges without lateral teeth, and an oval outline. They usually are white and have a slight-to-moderate bend at the posterior end. Small, empty shells of *M. balthica* and *M. calcarea* are frequently found intertidally; both may have a pink shell interior. *M. nasuta*, the Bent-Nose Clam, is larger (to 9 centimeters (3½ inches) in length); its posterior end is flattened and rather strongly bent to one side. Identifying species of *Macoma* often requires examination of muscle scars left on the interior valve surfaces. The specimen in the photo on page 31 shows a hole bored by a predatory gastropod.

117   *Protothaca staminea* — Steamer Clam, Little-Neck Clam

Length of shell to 7.6 centimeters (3 inches); height about three-fourths length; oval. Beak tends toward anterior end. With prominent radial ribs and concentric lines. Hinge has 3 stout teeth in each valve. Exterior of shell is rusty gray-white, sometimes mottled; interior, white. Individuals found in the low intertidal or shallow subtidal zones are usually less than 5 centimeters (2 inches) in length and are more often than not eroded in the beak area; specimens occurring in deeper water are less eroded and reach a larger size.

From Baja California to at least Cook Inlet. Mid- or low intertidal to shallow subtidal. Burrows in rubble, gravel or sand. An important edible clam in Alaska, *it is sometimes toxic, especially during summer months when it concentrates toxin from a planktonic organism it ingests.*

118   *Humilaria kennerleyi*

Length of shell to about 10 centimeters (4 inches); height equal to about three-fourths length. Shell with sharp concentric ridges whose edges bend toward the beak of the shell. Interior margin finely toothed. Shell heavy, chalky; exterior, gray-white; interior, white.

From the Kenai Peninsula and probably the south side of the Alaska Peninsula to central California. Strictly subtidal. In sand and sand-shell debris in 5-40 meters (3-22 fathoms). Frequently preyed upon by the sea stars *Orthasterias koehleri* and *Pycnopodia helianthoides*.

119 *Saxidomus giganteus* — Butter Clam

Length to about 10 centimeters (4 inches); height about three-fourths length. Beak is closer to the anterior than the posterior end. Hinge has 4 teeth in each valve. Ligament is large. Shell is heavy and marked externally by fine concentric lines. Valves gape slightly at posterior end. Exterior of valves is white, sometimes tinged with rusty brown or with a color similar to that of the material in which the clam is found; interior, white.

From the Aleutian Islands to central California. Low intertidal to shallow subtidal. In fine gravel or sand. May live 20 years or more. It is an important food clam in Alaska, *but may be toxic — especially during summer months — when it concentrates a toxin derived from a planktonic organism it ingests.* Subtidally preyed upon by the sea star *Pycnopodia helianthoides,* which digs it out of the gravel or sand.

120 *Mya truncata*

Length of shell to about 9 centimeters (3½ inches); height about two-thirds length. Valves are thin, slightly unequal in size and covered by a thin, olive-drab periostracum that cracks off easily. Shell has a large gape at the truncate posterior end. Inside of left valve has a horizontally projecting shelf near the hinge. Siphon is long and encased in a rough, gritty extension of the periostracum. Shell, white.

From the Arctic Ocean to Washington. Intertidal and shallow subtidal. In mud-sand. Often uncovered when digging for butter or steamer clams. Preyed upon by walrus, king eider ducks, arctic foxes and some species of fish. Other species of *Mya* also occur commonly in Alaskan waters; most have shells similar to that of *M. truncata,* but which gape only slightly at the posterior end and are not truncate.

121 *Hiatella arctica*

Length of shell to about 3.8 centimeters (1½ inches); height about one-half length; beak about one-third the total length from the anterior end. Posterior of shell may gape. Young specimens are nearly rectangular, but adults are twisted and misshapen. The hinge of young adults has two teeth. Exterior is chalky white with irregular growth lines; periostracum, gray to tan, thin and flaky.

From the Arctic Ocean to Panama. Intertidal to deep water.

Nestles in rock crevices or in kelp holdfasts. Often fouls salt-water pipelines.

122   *Entodesma saxicola* — Northwest Ugly Clam

Length of shell to about 15.2 centimeters (6 inches). Irregular and misshapen, generally oblong. Posterior end flaring and gaping. Hinge without teeth. Exterior is often eroded and encrusted; periostracum thick, rough, brown and flakes off when dry; interior pearly, tan to white.

From southern California to at least as far north as Prince William Sound. Found in shallow subtidal zones. Lives in crevices of rocks and grows to fit the cavity in which it has settled. Secretes byssal threads. The shell usually fractures when dried.

Class Cephalopoda — Octopuses and Squids

Cephalopods are among the most advanced of all invertebrates. Their neurosensory structures are highly developed and their nervous systems are equally complex. Because their brains are large and differentiated, they have the ability to discriminate and learn. They have several chemo- and tactile receptors, but their most remarkable sense organ is the eye, which in some species rivals that of man in its complexity and capability to form a clear, detailed image.

Squids, octopuses, cuttlefish, and *Nautilus* — the modern cephalopods — are the survivors of an ancient group, whose members are known in large part only from fossil records. They have largely evolved away from having the shell characteristic of most molluscs. Only *Nautilus,* a genus found in warm waters, retains an obvious external shell, one that can be distinguished from other molluscan shells by partitions that divide it into numerous internal chambers. The shell of a squid or cuttlefish is internal, while the octopus has no shell at any stage of its development.

Cephalopods are soft-bodied and have a large head which, in the process of development, fuses with the foot. For this reason they are called cephalopods, or "head-foot" animals. Extending from the cephalopod's head region are its arms —

ten in the case of most squids and eight for octopuses. These are equipped with powerful suction disks that can be used for clinging to substrate or for capturing prey. The cephalopod's body is protected by a mantle. In a squid the mantle projects forward as a collar around the head, and in an octopus it adheres to the surface of the head, making head and body appear as one.

Squids and octopuses have special pigment cells in their covering tissue that allow them to change color rapidly. Color, and sometimes texture, may be altered to blend with the surrounding background or to express a reaction to external stimuli. Squids and octopuses can also eject a cloud of sepia from the anus. This brown ink may protect the cephalopod by creating a visible distraction or possibly by affecting a predator's sense of smell in such a way that it cannot locate the prey.

Squids and octopuses can swim by forcibly ejecting water from the mantle cavity through a tube-shaped siphon. When swimming in this manner, octopuses always lead with their heads, but squids can change the direction of their siphons and dart forward or backward. In addition to this jetlike method of propulsion, squids swim by undulating two fleshy fins, one located on each side of the body. Webbed areas between the upper part of the octopus's arms permit it to glide if the arms are spread and the web is taut. Most squid are pelagic, but octopuses, although capable of swimming, are primarily bottom-dwellers that creep over the sea floor on their sucker-equipped arms.

Many squids and octopuses are nocturnal, staying hidden by day and emerging at night to seek food. Diet varies with species, but cephalopods generally feed on fish, other molluscs, and crustaceans. Captured food is brought to the mouth by the arms, then attacked by heavily muscled, horny jaws that may fit together like the two parts of a parrot's beak. Some cephalopods typically kill prey with a single bite, while others use venom to immobilize it.

In cephalopods the sexes are separate. One of the arms of the male is specially modified for the transfer of sperm to the female. Egg masses or single eggs are usually attached to rock or other hard surfaces, but some pelagic species have drifting eggs. Squid eggs are often surrounded by a gelatinous mass that protects them and makes them unpalatable to most animals. Thus, they can be left to hatch unattended. In contrast, the eggs of an octopus are usually tended by the female, who guards and ventilates them with jets of water to keep them clean.

Squid

123 *Rossia pacifica*

Total length to about 10 centimeters (4 inches). With 8 short, thick arms, and 2 long, slender tentacular arms that can be withdrawn into special pits. Body is smooth, short and stubby. The mantle is free all around. Fins are almost as long as the mantle, semi-circular and free at anterior. Often red-brown, but changeable in color due to presence of chromatophores.

From Baja California to Southeastern Alaska. Found from shallow subtidal zone to as deep as 550 meters (300 fathoms). A bottom dweller, but will swim short distances. It ejects ink if disturbed, and often the only indication of its presence is a blob of brown ink suspended in the water near bottom, a sign that an animal was there but is gone. Feeds on small crustaceans. Eggs are deposited in clusters on undersides of rocks; each egg has a white, onion-shaped covering. Incubation is slow; more than a year may elapse between egg deposition and hatching.

Octopus

124 *Octopus dofleini*

Arm-spread to as much as 3 meters (10 feet). Weight to 45 kilograms (100 pounds) or more. With 8 arms. Body and head covered by mantle. Siphon located below head at edge of mantle. Arms 3-5 times the length of the body; on males the tip of third right arm is modified for deposition of sperm. Body has extensive skin folds and papillae.

From the Bering Sea to Baja California. Low intertidal to 180 meters (98 fathoms) or more. Territorial; usually found in dens dug out under boulders or in crevices in bedrock; sites are identifiable by an accumulation of crustacean or mollusc shells. Feeds on fish, echinoderms, molluscs, and crustaceans including king, Dungeness, and tanner crabs. In turn it is prey to halibut and sea lions. Uses venom to immobilize prey and a radula to rasp holes in shells. Breeding occurs from winter to spring. The eggs are oval, with a filament at one end. Using these filaments, females secure eggs into bunches and attach them to the substrate. When females begin to spawn, they cease hunting and devote their time to tending the eggs and protecting them from predators. The female apparently dies before the eggs hatch. The larvae are planktonic. Only one other octopus, *Octopus leioderma*, is common in Alaskan waters; it occurs only in deep water and can be distinguished from *O. dofleini* by its smooth body surface.

Phylum: Annelida

The Segmented Worms

The annelids, a phylum of about 8,000 species, are well represented on land as well as in marine and fresh waters. Perhaps the most familiar annelids are the common earthworms. They, like all other members of the phylum, have bodies that are transversely divided into many similar segments. It is this segmentation that most readily distinguishes annelids from all other worms or wormlike animals.

In addition to being segmented, annelids are soft-bodied and bilaterally symmetrical. The head of an annelid, which may be simple or have ornate sensory organs and feeding structures, usually consists of two parts, the second of which surrounds the animal's mouth. Typically, the segments of an annelid bear chitinous setae or remnants of these structures. Internally, these animals have a closed circulatory system, a ventral nerve cord, an excretory system and a digestive system.

Annelids are divided into three classes — the Oligochaeta, the Hirundinea, and the Polychaeta. The Polychaeta is the largest group. Its members occur primarily in marine waters and differ from species of other annelids by usually having parapodia with numerous setae and a head region with well-developed appendages. The Oligochaeta includes terrestrial earthworms, many fresh-water species, and some species that live in marine habitats. Oligochaetes usually have small heads without appendages, and their body segments lack parapodia. As a rule they have few setae. The Hirundinea, or leeches, live primarily in fresh water but there are some species in the sea and on land. Leeches are generally flattened top to bottom and have an anterior and a posterior sucker. The anterior sucker surrounds the mouth, which helps some species draw blood from hosts.

Class Polychaeta — Segmented Marine Worms

Polychaetes are a diverse group. Some are small, but others are more than 1 meter (39 inches) in length. Parapodia, the fleshy, lateral outgrowths which aid in locomotion may be well developed or minimal. Polychaetes may be equipped with large chitinous jaws, scales that cover the dorsal surface, long sensory antennae or brightly colored feathery structures. Their diversity in form has enabled polychaetes to exploit a wide range of habitats and is closely linked to their diverse feeding and reproductive habits.

These worms can be divided into two groups — the Errantia and the Sedentaria. Errant polychaetes are generally active and may live in colonies of other invertebrates, move freely over the sea floor, swim in the water column, or live in burrows. They usually have clearly defined heads with well-developed sense organs and large parapodia. Sedentary

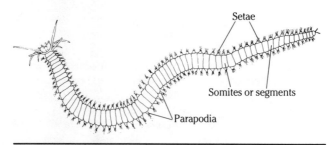

Figure 14. Polychaete, dorsal view

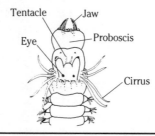

Figure 15. Polychaete, dorsal view of head with proboscis extended.

polychaetes usually live in secreted tubes they make themselves. They are less active than the Errant polychaetes and their heads are less clearly differentiated. Their sense organs and parapodia are generally reduced.

In Alaskan waters, polychaetes occur in a wide variety of habitats from the intertidal zone down to great depths. Although ubiquitous, many are small and often inconspicuous.

Feeding methods among polychaetes are as varied as the habitats in which they are found. Many errant polychaetes are predatory and feed on small crustaceans, molluscs or other annelids. They often catch their prey with hooklike jaws borne on an eversible pharynx. Burrowing polychaetes feed by swallowing mud and digesting the organic material it contains. Tube-building worms are often equipped with elaborate, feathery cirri that are extended to collect small particles of food from the surrounding water.

Reproductive behavior is also varied and sometimes quite bizarre. The sexes are usually separate. Some species release eggs and sperm into the water, where fertilization occurs; others attach clusters of eggs to hard surfaces. A number of polychaetes brood their young, and still others routinely reproduce asexually by budding off new individuals from specialized body segments. Some polychaetes produce special reproductive forms, called epitokes, by transformation of a non-breeding animal or by budding off one or more new, breeding individuals from a non-breeding parent. Some epitokes attain a large size and are equipped with parapodia that enable them to swim and to occur in swarms at the water's surface during breeding seasons.

125 *Nephtys* sp.

Length to about 20.3 centimeters (8 inches). The body is thick and elongate; segments short. The head has 4 small tentacles, usually without eyes. Parapodia are bilobed, with gills between them. Usually cream colored.

Various species of *Nephtys* are found in Alaskan waters. Intertidal and shallow subtidal; usually burrowed into sand-mud. Predatory. Similar in superficial appearance to *Nereis,* but the head is distinctly different. *Nephtys* has a complex ligamentary system that facilitates efficient crawling and swimming.

126 *Nereis brandti*

Length occasionally to 91 centimeters (3 feet) or more, commonly to about 40.6 centimeters (16 inches). Head has 4 eyes, 1 pair of antennae, 4 pairs of long cirri; has 2 large jaws on an eversible pharynx. Body segments have large, bilobed parapodia that bear numerous setae. Dorsal surface is an iridescent blue-green; ventral surface, paler.

Occurs from at least Southeastern Alaska to southern California. Low intertidal and subtidal. May be found on mud or sand; often burrows. Uses jaws to tear algae on which it feeds. Capable of swimming; swarms at the water's surface when spawning. Several other species of *Nereis* occur in Alaskan waters. *N. vexillosa,* which is frequently found intertidally, has variable coloration, but is usually blue or green to gray, and has a maximum length of about 25.4 centimeters (10 inches).

127 ? *Harmothoe* sp. — Scale Worm

Species of *Harmothoe* have a body that is relatively short, with no more than 50 segments. Each of the parapodia has 2 bundles of long setae. The dorsal surface of the worm has 15 overlapping pairs of scales forming nearly a complete cover.

Numerous species of scale worms occur in Alaskan marine waters. Many are free-living, but some occur commensally with other invertebrates, especially with sea stars. If a scale worm lives with a sea star, it is most often found on the oral side of the host, either on the central disk or nestled between the bases of adjacent rays. Scale worms are generally carnivorous. Some species brood eggs beneath the scales. The specimen in the photo on page 33 is missing scales on the posterior portion of the body.

128 *Trypanosyllis* sp.

Length to about 20.3 centimeters (8 inches) or more. The body is elongate and slender, usually with many crowded segments. Head has 3 tentacles and 4 eyes. Each parapodia has one long, beaded dorsal cirrus and a shorter ventral cirrus.

Occurs from the Aleutian Islands and Kodiak to California. They are predatory and often found with sponges. Some reproduce asexually by budding off new individuals.

129 Family Terebellidae

Length usually over 5 centimeters (2 inches). The head has

numerous, threadlike tentacles that can be extended but cannot be withdrawn into the mouth. Lives in a secreted tube that can be slender and translucent, covered with mucus or mud, or inlaid with sand grains or shell fragments; tubes are usually attached to a substrate such as rock or algae.

Species of *Terebellidae* are recorded from Arctic to Southeastern Alaska. The bodies are seen less often than are their tentacles, which look like thin spaghetti and may radiate 10 inches or more from each tube. These worms are deposit feeders that convey material to the mouth along the ciliated groove running the length of each tentacle. Terebellids, free of tubes, may occasionally be seen in midwater.

130 *Pectinaria granulata*

Length to about 3.8 centimeters (1½ inches). Secretes a slightly bent, conical tube into which coarse sand grains are added. Anterior end of worm possesses stout, golden setae.

Occurs from Southeastern Alaska to Puget Sound. Low intertidal to about 250 meters (137 fathoms); strictly subtidal in southern end of range. Lives upside down in mud and feeds by shoveling material into the mouth with the stout setae. The photograph on page 34 shows only the tube of the animal.

131 *Spiochaetopterus costarum* — Tube Worm

Length to about 61 centimeters (24 inches); diameter to about 3 millimeters (⅛ inch). Body is divided into 3 regions by structural differences in the parapodia. Head has 2 long, spirally coiled, tentacular sense organs. Secretes a chitinous, translucent tube marked by closely spaced rings.

Occurs from California to Southeastern Alaska. Subtidal. Tubes are often covered by algae and small invertebrates.

132 *Schizobranchia* sp. — Feather-duster Worm

Length to about 15.2 centimeters (6 inches). Secretes a chitinous tube that is thick at the base, thinner at the top, opaque and horn-colored. Feeding cirri form a feathery crown and branch up to 6 times. Cirri are tan with numerous large eyes on the back side of each primary stem.

Species of *Schizobranchia* occur from Southeastern Alaska to Central America. Low intertidal and shallow subtidal in rocky habitats. Filter feeders. Tubes are often hidden by a growth of algae or invertebrates such as hydroids or sea squirts. More than one species probably occurs in Alaskan waters. Although many specimens have tan to nearly colorless feeding cirri, some have crimson or wine-colored cirri.

133   *Spirorbis* sp. — Tube Worm
Length of body less than 6 millimeters (¼ inch). Builds a coiling, white, calcareous tube less than 3 millimeters (⅛ inch) in total diameter. Feeding cirri form a feathery crown, often orange to red. Tube aperture can be sealed with a minute operculum, which is a modified cirrus.

Several species of *Spirorbis* may occur in shallow Alaskan waters from the Arctic to Southeastern Alaska, but distinguishing one from another involves careful work with a microscope. All species occur cemented to surfaces such as rocks, mollusc shells, or algae and feed by extending cirri to collect microscopic plankton from the water.

134   *Crucigera* sp. — Tube Worm
Length to about 5 centimeters (2 inches). Builds a large, irregulary coiling, white, calcareous tube. Feeding cirri, which form a feathery crown, are cross-banded with red and white. Base of operculum has 2 rounded knobs that may be bilobed.

Species of *Crucigera* occur in Alaska from at least Unalaska to the southeastern sector of the state. Intertidal and shallow subtidal. Filter feeders. They are found cemented to hard surfaces and often in groups. Tubes are frequently covered with algae or other growth so that only the most recently constructed portion appears white. These tube worms are very similar to *Serpula* but may be distinguished by the shape of the operculum.

135   *Serpula vermicularis* — Tube Worm
Length to about 10 centimeters (4 inches). Builds a sinuous, calcareous tube; feeding cirri form a feathery crown and are usually either solid red or cross-banded with crimson and white. The operculum is shaped like a broad funnel, striped with red and white and lacks knoblike processes.

Occurs from Prince William Sound to California. Low intertidal and shallow subtidal. Filter feeder. Often found in groups.
Tubes are frequently covered with algae and other growth.
Feeding cirri retract rapidly if the worm is disturbed. The
shape of the operculum distinguishes it from *Crucigera*.

Class Hirundinea — Leeches

About 300 species of leeches have been described. Most of
these live in fresh water but a few are found in marine habitats
or on land. About a half-dozen marine species occur along the
Alaskan coast.

Contrary to common belief, leeches are not all parasites,
although many species do draw blood from animals to which
they are temporarily or more or less permanently attached.
Some leeches are predators or scavengers.

In appearance, leeches are usually somewhat flattened,
although some may be cylindrical. Their bodies usually taper
anteriorly. They range from about 1.3 centimeters (½ inch) in
length to 0.5 meter (19 inches) or more. The body is divided
into 34 segments, but it appears to have many more divisions
because each segment may be superficially subdivided. The
head is somewhat distinct and has a mouth sucker. Eyes are
located on the head and their number, position and form are
important in species identification. The posterior end of the
body usually bears a second sucker.

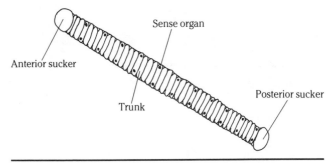

Figure 16. Leech

Leeches move like the caterpillars called inchworms. The
body is extended, the mouth sucker is attached to a surface,

and the posterior part of the body is pulled forward. When the posterior sucker is attached, the head sucker is freed and the movement begins again. In addition to creeping in this manner, some marine leeches swim by undulating movements.

Leeches are hermaphroditic. Eggs may be carried externally by the parent, deposited on a firm surface, or encapsulated in a protective case that is attached to a surface.

136   *Notostomobdella cyclostoma*

Length to about 12 centimeters (4¾ inches). Slender when fully extended, flattened when contracted. Sucker on head is broad, sometimes exceeding the width of the body. Without visible eyes. Posterior sucker may expand to a diameter greater than that of the mouth sucker and is more deeply cupped. White to cream with darker blotches.

Bristol Bay and the Pribilof Islands to Southeastern Alaska. Shallow subtidal to at least 366 meters (200 fathoms). Most frequently collected where the bottom is muddy. Often found adhering to the shell of the king crab *Paralithodes camtschatica*. Egg capsules may also be found on the king crab; they are brown and about 0.6 centimeter (¼ inch) in diameter, circular or elliptical in outline, and flattened. Although *N. cyclostoma* is frequently found on king crabs, its relationship to the crab is unclear. It may be a free-living, predaceous species that attaches to prey only when feeding. Specimens of *N. cyclostoma* have also been found attached to skates, sculpins and other fishes, and to tanner crabs.

Phylum: Sipuncula

The Peanut Worms

Sipunculans, or peanut worms, are strictly marine animals. Although the phylum includes only about 100 species, members may be found from the intertidal zone to great depths in both cold and warm waters. In Alaska sipunculans are not well studied, but at least three species are known to occur there.

The body of a peanut worm is bilaterally symmetrical, lacks

segmentation, and is divided into two parts — an anterior section called the introvert and a fatter posterior portion called the trunk. The introvert can be completely pulled into the trunk, turning outside-in.

Externally, a sipunculan has few striking features. At the anterior tip of the introvert is the animal's mouth, an opening surrounded by simple or branching tentacles. The surface of the introvert may have hooks or spines, and the body surface in general may be smooth or rough.

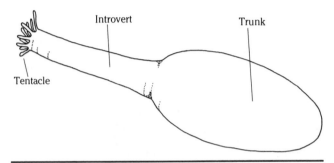

Figure 17. Sipunculid

Peanut worms are sedentary animals that burrow into sand or mud or wedge themselves into crevices, empty shells, or other tight places. When burrowing, a sipunculan extends its introvert, expands it at the tip and pulls the body forward then by shortening the introvert. To feed they usually sort through sand or mud to remove organic debris and other food.

Sexes are separate, and eggs and sperm are released into the sea where fertilization occurs. Larvae are free-swimming until they settle and transform into adults.

137 *Phascolosoma agassizii*

Length, when fully extended, to about 14 centimeters (5½ inches). Tentacles are small and fingerlike. Anterior end of introvert has 15-25 circles of minute hooks. Body surface roughened by numerous conical papillae. Body wall opaque to slightly translucent; gray to dark brown, often irregularly marked by bands or patches of dark color; many individuals have a dark trunk and a lighter introvert, the latter marked by irregular dark bands or patches.

From Kodiak Island to Baja California. Most frequently found in the low intertidal zone but also to subtidal depths of 201 meters (110 fathoms). Found in mussel beds, under rocks lying on sand or mud, burrowing in sand or mud, and in rock crevices.

138   *Golfingia margaritacea*

Length to about 7.6 centimeters (3 inches) when extended. With 16 or fewer tentacles, the number of tentacles increasing with the size of the specimen. Introvert equal to half the total body length or less. No spines nor hooks on introvert. Skin smooth, pale and translucent.

Circumpolar; south from Alaska to British Columbia and perhaps Puget Sound. Buries itself in soft substrate or nestles in crevices. May occur in low intertidal zone.

Phylum: Arthropoda

The Barnacles, Shrimps, Crabs and their Allies

The phylum Arthropoda is the largest of all animal phyla and includes several hundred thousand species. Its members are found on land, in fresh and salt water, in the air, and as parasites on many animals, including man. No other group of organisms has adapted so successfully to such a broad variety of habitats.

Arthropods are characterized by a chitinous body covering called an exoskeleton. They are bilaterally symmetrical with segmented bodies. Their appendages are jointed and some may be specialized for specific functions.

To grow, arthropods must shed their exoskeletons periodically and form new ones. In the complex process of molting, a soft exoskeleton is formed beneath the old one. When the new exoskeleton is sufficiently developed, the old body covering splits and the temporarily soft animal emerges and expands to a larger size. At this point, the animal is vulnerable to predators and may seek a secluded hiding place until the new exoskeleton hardens. Because growth tends to be greater in young organisms, many arthropods molt more frequently in early life.

Among the major classes of arthropods, insects (Insecta)

and spiders (Arachnida) are primarily terrestrial or fresh-water animals. Members of some smaller classes, such as the pycnogonids (Pycnogonida) and the horseshoe crabs (Merostomata), are marine, but the majority of marine arthropods belong to the class Crustacea, that includes barnacles, shrimps, crabs, copepods, mysids, and amphipods.

Crustaceans are diverse in their forms and habits, but most are aquatic and have gills for respiration. All have a pair of mandibles (mouth parts capable of biting or chewing) and two pairs of antennae included in their set of head appendages. Sexes are separate.

Subclass Cirripedia — Barnacles

Barnacles may be found on rocks, pilings, boat hulls, kelp, mollusc shells, or pieces of driftwood. Even animals such as crabs, shrimps, and whales provide a surface for barnacle growth. Some barnacles, highly modified and bearing little resemblance to their more conventional relatives, are parasitic on crustaceans, ascidians and other animals.

Unlike most crustaceans, barnacles are hermaphroditic. Cross fertilization is the usual way of reproducing, but if a barnacle is isolated, it presumably is self-fertilizing. Barnacle eggs are brooded in the adult's mantle cavity and hatch into larvae called nauplii that leave the sedentary parent to swim free. After several molts, the nauplius become a cypris larva with a bivalved shell. This larva in turn becomes attached to a suitable substrate by cementing itself head down with a secreted adhesive. In typical transition to adult form, the bivalved shell is shed and the calcareous plates that will surround the adult begin to form.

Excluding the parasitic members of the Cirripedia, two kinds of barnacles may be found in Alaskan waters. Gooseneck barnacles, which attach to a surface by a leathery stalk, are sometimes found pelagically on drifting wood or other materials. Acorn barnacles are far more common; they attach without a stalk, often have a conical shell, and occur abundantly on rocky shores.

The sides of the acorn barnacle's shell are usually made up of six interlocking calcareous plates. Two additional pairs of movable cover plates close the opening at the top of the shell when the tide is out and when predators threaten. The shell base of many acorn barnacles is calcareous, but in some species it is membranous.

To feed, a sedentary barnacle extends feathery cirri, the transformed thoracic appendages of the cypris larva, through a slit between the cover plates. With a sweeping motion, the cirri comb the water for food particles that will be carried inside the shell and toward the mouth. If the barnacle is undisturbed, the rhythmic sweeping of the cirri continues steadily with many cycles per minute.

Like other crustaceans, barnacles molt in order to grow. In molting, the membranous covering of the soft animal is shed and replaced. Periodically, the surface of inshore waters may be abundantly covered with filmy, discarded molts, or casts. The hard calcareous covering of the barnacle is never shed, but its size increases as the soft animal inside grows.

Barnacles frequently fall prey to a variety of other marine invertebrates. Several snails, including *Nucella lamellosa* and *Ceratostoma foliatum,* are known to feed on barnacles. Sometimes areas of barnacles may be heavily preyed upon by the small nudibranch *Lamellidoris fusca.* Also taking their toll of barnacle populations are sea stars, such as *Evasterias troschelii, Leptasterias hexactis,* and *Pisaster ochraceus,* and birds such as crows and some of the diving ducks.

Acorn Barnacles

139 *Balanus nubilus*

Diameter to about 10 centimeters (4 inches); height to 7 centimeters (2¾ inches) or more. Base of shell irregularly porous. The upper opening surrounding the cover plates is large, with a jagged, rough edge. Beak of cover plates is large and hooked. Shell exterior, dirty white; interior of cover plates, buff.

From Southeastern Alaska to central California. Subtidal to about 55 meters (30 fathoms), often in 10 meters (5.5 fathoms) or less. It is the largest barnacle on the Pacific Coast of North America. Usually heavily encrusted. Often found in groups, with some individuals growing on others. Empty shells may serve as living spaces for small shrimps, crabs, and fishes. One fish, the grunt sculpin, backs into the empty shells. Its head mimics the beak of the missing barnacle.

140 *Balanus cariosus*

Diameter to about 5 centimeters (2 inches); height to about 8.2

centimeters (3¼ inches). Size and shape variable; uncrowded shells are conical with sides covered by numerous, down-pointing spines; crowded shells may be tubular and lack spines; cover plates form a sharp point. Shell with a membranous, rather than calcareous, base. Usually dirty gray; young individuals and new growth are white.

From the Aleutian Islands to California. Most common in the mid-intertidal zone. Often locally abundant. It is the largest common intertidal barnacle in Alaska. It can usually be identified by its covering of spines. *Balanus balanoides* also has a membranous, rather than calcareous, base, but it has no exterior spines and its cover plates are not sharply pointed.

141 *Balanus glandula*

Diameter to about 1.9 centimeters (¾ inch) when uncrowded; height about equal to diameter. Base of shell is calcareous; edge of base may be minutely scalloped. Shell, gray; new growth, white; lining of cover plates, jet black. Black coloration shows through each of the 2 larger, more flattened cover plates as a single, dark triangle.

From the Aleutian Islands to Baja California. Mid-intertidal. Often in dense aggregations. Shell shape varies with environmental conditions, especially with the degree of crowding. *B. balanoides* is similar and is often mixed with *B. glandula*. *B. balanoides* has a membranous shell base and a dark lining to the cover plates. On the two larger plates this shows through as two triangular streaks. *Chthamalus dalli*, another intertidal barnacle, is distinguished by cover plates that form a distinctive cross where they meet.

Gooseneck Barnacle

142 *Lepas pacifica*

Total length of animal, including stalk, about 3.2 centimeters (1¼ inches). With 5 thin plates marked by fine radial lines; the dark color of soft animal is visible through the plates. Base of carina (the long, slender plate that runs nearly the length of the barnacle excluding the stalk) is expanded on each side to form a "T." Plates, white; stalk, yellow-brown.

Alaska to California; pelagic, on driftwood or floating kelp.

L. anatifera is a similar species but has thicker plates with no color of the soft animal showing through them; the base of its carina is more like a "Y" than a "T," and the edge of the orifice is bright orange.

Superorder Peracarida — Mysids, Amphipods, Isopods, and Their Allies

Peracarids include a number of subgroups of crustaceans sharing common characteristics. In each, the first segment of the thorax is fused to the head, and other thoracic segments may be fused to the complex. The carapace is an outgrowth of the posterior margin of the head; it may cover the whole thorax, but it does not fuse with more than four segments. Female peracarids have a brood pouch in the thoracic region.

As a whole the peracarids are well represented in Alaskan waters, but they are generally small and often overlooked. They may be difficult to identify by species without the use of a microscope and an expert's help. In northern waters, mysids, amphipods and isopods are the more commonly observed members of the group.

Mysids are almost exclusively marine and include about 450 species. They are shrimplike in appearance and usually about 1.9-3.2 centimeters (¾-1¼ inches) long. Most of the thoracic region of a mysid is covered by a carapace, but only three of the thoracic segments are fused to it. Most mysids are filter feeders, but some are scavengers. Sexes are separate and eggs are brooded in the special pouch until they are juveniles resembling the parents. Mysids occur from the intertidal zone down to great depths and may live on the sea floor or in open water. They are sometimes abundant and often serve as food for fishes and other marine animals.

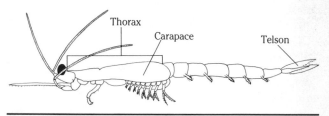

Figure 18. Mysid

Isopods include several thousand species and occur in marine and fresh waters and on land. They may be free-living or parasitic. An isopod lacks a carapace and is flattened dorsoventrally. Isopods have well-developed legs on the thorax and walk in the manner similar to that of insects. Some can also swim. Isopods may be scavengers, herbivores or predators. Sexes are separate and the young are well developed when set free from the female's brood pouch.

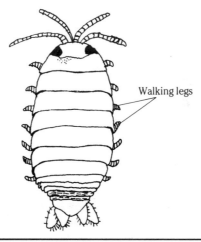

Walking legs

Figure 19. Isopod, dorsal view

Amphipods have no carapace and are flattened from side to side. The first, or both the first and second, thoracic segments unite with the head. The amphipod's back is normally convex in shape and by flexing strong muscles, the animal can straighten its back to leap or hop. Sexes are separate. Eggs develop in the female's brood pouch and may remain there until the female molts and the exoskeleton, including plates of the brood pouch, is cast off.

Amphipods, sometimes called beach hoppers or sand fleas, may be abundant from the high intertidal zone to deep sub-tidal waters. They may be herbivores or carnivores, those in the latter group being predators, scavengers or filter feeders. Amphipods are primarily marine animals and usually bottom dwellers, although many are strong swimmers. Amphipods are familiar to long line fishermen who lose bait and hooked fish to them.

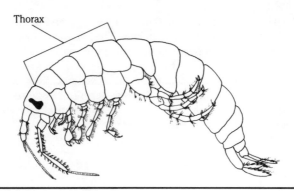

Figure 20. Amphipod

Mysid

143 *Neomysis mercedis*

Length to about 2.5 centimeters (1 inch). The telson (the terminal, flap-like portion of the abdomen) is without a cleft; telson about twice as long as wide. Translucent with dark markings.

From Prince William Sound to California. May be found on sand in shallow, often brackish water; sometimes at creek mouths. A number of mysid species occur in Alaskan waters. Identification to species requires a microscope.

Isopod

144 *Gnorimosphaeroma oregonensis*

Length to about 1.3 centimeters (½ inch). The body is flattened from top to bottom. Telson (terminal segment of the abdomen) is not deeply notched nor divided into three lobes. A dull shade of green or brown, often mottled.

From Southcentral Alaska to California. Intertidal. Most frequently found in areas of fresh water seepage where sand or other gritty materials collect in small pockets. Because it is capable of rolling into a ball, it is often called a pillbug. A number of other isopods, some with shapes different from that of *Gnorimosphaeroma*, occur in Alaska's intertidal and shallow subtidal waters.

Amphipods

145 *Orchestia traskiana*

Length to about 1.9 centimeters (¾ inch). Fourth segment of the first pincer-like thoracic appendage of the male has a small, posterior, translucent projection. Light salmon-pink to gray.

From Southeastern Alaska to California. Found under debris on sandy and muddy shores and in salt marshes; generally at higher levels of the intertidal zone. It may easily be confused with similar intertidal amphipods; only microscopic examination of small structures will clearly distinguish one species from another.

146 *Anonyx* sp.

Length to about 3.8 centimeters (1½ inches). Body moderately slender with well-developed marginal plates that partially cover the appendages. Exoskeleton, hard and smooth. Eyes, kidney-shaped. Light tan with dark eyes.

Species of *Anonyx* are difficult to differentiate. One species, *A. nugax,* is circumpolar, occurs south to California, and is found from the intertidal zone to depths of 183 meters (100 fathoms) or more. Species of *Anonyx* are usually subtidal. They may be carnivorous, voracious, and aggressive. Sand fleas of this genus often destroy bait and hooked fish on long lines.

Order Decapoda — Shrimps and Crabs

Decapod crustaceans are easily recognized by the 10 legs (5 pairs) located on the cephalothorax (the part of the body formed by the union of the head and thorax). At least the first pair is usually modified into chelipeds, or pincers, not used for locomotion. The cephalothorax is covered by a continuous exoskeleton called a carapace. All members of the Decapoda fall into one of two subgroups, the Natantia, or swimming decapods, and the Reptantia, or crawling decapods.

Members of the Natantia include the shrimps. These animals have large, muscular abdomens terminating in tail fans. Their bodies are generally flattened from side to side.

The first five pairs of abdominal appendages are well developed and modified for swimming. Many members of the Natantia also have a long rostrum, a pointed extension of the carapace directed forward from between the animal's eyes. Shrimp are represented in Alaskan waters by more than 60 species, some of which are large and commercially important.

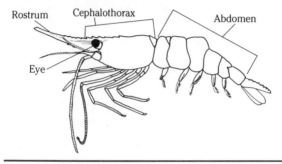

Figure 21. Shrimp

In contrast to the shrimps, members of the Reptantia have bodies flattened from top to bottom and rostrums which are usually small. The first five abdominal appendages are also small or entirely absent; they do not aid in swimming. Members of two reptantian subgroups, the Anomura and the Brachyura, occur in Alaskan waters.

The anomurans are the hermit crabs, king crabs and their

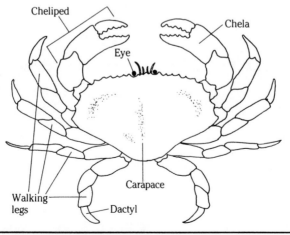

Figure 22. A brachyuran crab, dorsal view

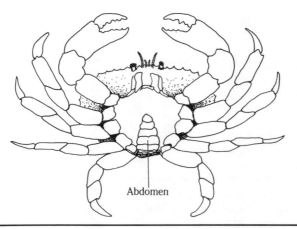

Abdomen

Figure 23. A brachyuran crab, ventral view

relatives. They have one pair of chelipeds, three pairs of functional walking legs, and a fifth pair of small thoracic appendages usually drawn under the rear edge of the carapace. The abdomen is well developed and may be soft and delicate or partially covered with hard plates. Among the hermit crabs, abdomens are long and soft and usually curved or spirally coiled. The unique appendages of the abdomen anchor them in the empty snail shells or worm tubes in which the crabs live. In other anomurans, such as Alaska's familiar king crab, the abdomen is flaplike and folded under the crab's cephalothorax. Female anomurans carry their eggs on the abdominal appendages until they hatch.

Brachyuran crabs are the most highly evolved crustaceans. They have four pairs of walking legs and one pair of chelipeds. Their carapaces are usually broad and short. Their abdomens are small, heavily covered with protective plates, and characteristically tucked up against the lower surface of the cephalothorax. The male's abdomen is usually narrow and with only rudimentary appendages. The female's is broader and has four pairs of well-developed appendages used for carrying eggs.

Shrimps

147 *Pandalus borealis* — Pink Shrimp
Length (including rostrum) to about 16.5 centimeters

(6½ inches). Rostrum about 1.5-2 times as long as the cephalothorax, with dorsal spines that extend to the tip. Third abdominal segment bent at an angle, with a conspicuous dorsal ridge and dorsal spines on and in front of the rear margin. Fourth abdominal segment also has a dorsal spine at the posterior margin. When alive, translucent pink without distinctive markings.

Circumpolar; from the Arctic Ocean to northern Oregon. At depths of 50-600 meters (27-328 fathoms), but occasionally in 10 meters (5.5 fathoms) or less. Usually on mud or mud-sand. Lives about 5-6 years. Normally all individuals are protandric hermaphrodites; that is, they begin life as males and later become females. Developing eggs are carried on abdominal appendages of females for about 6 months and hatch in March or April. Larvae are planktonic for 2-3 months and settle to bottom when about 1.9 centimeters (¾ inch) long. Adults usually occur in great numbers, apparently staying in dense swarms. When they are seen on the sea floor most are oriented in the same direction if undisturbed, usually holding their tails into the current. At night, they may migrate upward into water column. They are active predators on small bottom-dwelling and open water invertebrates, especially crab larvae, and are an important food source for many fishes including salmon, halibut, cod, rockfish and sculpins. Because of their abundance, they are an important link to larger organisms in the food web. They are Alaska's most important commercial shrimp species.

148 *Pandalus goniurus* — Humpy

Length (including rostrum) to about 12 centimeters (4¾ inches). Rostrum 1.5 times as long as carapace, anterior half ascending and posterior half horizontal. No spines on anterior half; mid-dorsal surface abdomen's third segment has a blunt ridge and a distinct hump ahead of the rear margin. No spine on the dorsal posterior edge of the third or fourth abdominal segment. When alive, transparent to translucent with a prominent, thin, red line on the carapace, roughly paralleling the ventral and posterior edges; several similar lines on abdomen run obliquely upward from front to rear.

From the Chukchi Sea to Puget Sound. Subtidal from 6-100 meters (3-55 fathoms) or more. Usually on mud or mud-sand but occasionally found in shallow, rocky areas; distribution spotty but may be abundant locally. Remains on bottom during the day; at night may migrate upward into the water column to feed. It is an important prey species for many bottom-feeding fishes and makes up a small part of Alaska's commercial shrimp catch.

149   *Pandalus danae* — Dock Shrimp

Length (including rostrum) to about 15.2 centimeters (6 inches). Rostrum a little longer than carapace. Dorsal spines (8-12) on the cephalothorax, but do not extend behind the middle of the carapace. Third abdominal segment of abdomen not ridged. Red-brown to green with prominent brown lines on abdomen (lines run obliquely downward toward rear).

From central California to Cook Inlet; subtidal at depths of 1-200 meters (0.5-109 fathoms). Occurs in shallow waters wherever there are kelp and rock crevices. During the day it is normally backed into crevices with its rostrum and antennae protruding, but at night it leaves the hiding place to forage. Its life cycle similar to that of *P. borealis*. Feeds on a variety of bottom-dwelling invertebrates (snails, worms, limpets, shrimps, etc.) and on carrion. Serves as an important food for many bottom fishes, such as halibut, cod and sculpins, and for diving birds such as cormorants and mergansers. Perhaps the most commonly seen shrimp in Alaska because of its relatively large size and its abundance in very shallow waters. Commercially significant in British Columbia and Puget Sound, where it is called the coonstripe shrimp; incidental in Alaska's commercial shrimp catch.

150   *Pandalus hypsinotus* — Coonstripe Shrimp

Length (including rostrum) to about 20.3 centimeters (8 inches). Rostrum a little longer than the carapace, strongly dipped, then upturned at tip. Dorsal spines (17-21) on cephalothorax; some present behind the mid-carapace. Third abdominal segment without a spine or ridge. Irregular red spots on cephalothorax; broken bands of dark red on the abdomen and legs.

From Norton Sound to Washington. Usually in 50-200 meters (27-109 fathoms), but occasionally as shallow as 5 meters (2.7 fathoms) on rocks, mud or mud-sand; distribution spotty. Small individuals often migrate up into the water column at night. Life history is similar to that of *P. borealis*. An important prey species for many fish. May occur in commercial trawl catches and is caught in pots in rocky areas.

151 *Pandalus platyceros* — Spot Shrimp

Length (including rostrum) to about 27 centimeters (11 inches). Rostrum dips in front of eyes, then ascends again so that tip is above level of carapace. Dorsal spines on cephalothorax not present behind middle of carapace. Translucent orange with horizontal light bands on cephalothorax and a distinctive pair of white spots on the first and on the fifth abdominal segments; small individuals may be green, brown or orange, but the two pairs of spots on the abdomen are usually prominent.

From eastern Aleutian Islands to southern California. Subtidal at about 60-500 meters (33-273 fathoms). Found in rough, rocky areas, often where there are sheer rock cliffs. Juveniles to 1.5 years of age are common in areas of rock or kelp at 2-20 meters (1-11 fathoms). Life history similar to that of *P. borealis*. Feeds on bottom-dwelling invertebrates. Commercially valuable because of its size (large individuals weigh up to one-fourth pound); caught primarily by pot fishing in rocky areas; occurs only in small numbers in commercial trawl catches.

152 *Lebbeus groenlandicus*

Length (including rostrum) to about 7 centimeters (2¾ inches). Rostrum is narrow, flattened and elongate. Four large spines on dorsal midline of carapace; prominent marginal spines at lower, side edge of abdominal segments. Color variable, green to brown, with various mottlings.

From the Chukchi Sea to Puget Sound. Shallow subtidal to about 125 meters (68 fathoms). In shallow areas, often on kelp or rocks; when deeper, usually on sand-gravel. If undisturbed and resting on substrate, holds abdomen in a distinctive, elevated S-curve.

153 *Lebbeus grandimanus*

Length (including rostrum) to about 5 centimeters (2 inches). Transparent, with encircling bands of yellow and red alternating with purple markings on both cephalothorax and abdomen (regional differences occur in the arrangement and prominence of color bands); tail fan and appendages of cephalothorax marked with yellow.

From Amchitka Island in the Aleutian Islands to Puget Sound. Subtidal at about 10-30 meters (5.5-16.4 fathoms). Found in association with the anemone *Cribrinopsis fernaldi* (the anemone shown with *L. grandimanus* on the front cover and page 40) and occasionally with *Tealia crassicornis;* usually rests at the base of the anemone or perches on its column.

154 *Crangon* sp.

Length (including rostrum) to about 7.6 centimeters (3 inches). Rostrum is short, without spines, usually not as long as eyestalks. Body slightly flattened from top to bottom, and wider than high. Gray to gray-brown.

Several species of *Crangon* occur in Alaskan waters. Distinguishing one species from another requires careful examination, but the characteristics of the genus are easily observable. Often burrows into sand or mud, leaving only its eyes exposed. May migrate upward into water column at night to feed; often seen near the water's surface around lighted areas.

155 *Nectocrangon* sp.

Length to about 7.6 centimeters (3 inches). Similar in appearance to members of the genus *Crangon* but lacks a rostrum and has eyes that appear close set and nearly concealed by the carapace. Gray-brown with broad dark and light bands on abdomen and legs.

Several species of *Nectocrangon* occur in Alaskan waters. They are frequently taken in trawls but otherwise are not commonly seen. They occur at depths of 10 meters (5.5 fathoms) or more.

Anomuran Crabs

156 *Hapalogaster* sp.

Carapace length to about 3.2 centimeters (1¼ inches). Carapace, chelipeds, and legs flattened and very hairy. Lateral edges of carapace behind the cervical groove (an obvious groove that separates the fore area of the carapace from the lateral sector) have 5 spines that decrease in size posteriorly. Abdomen is soft, sacklike and not completely folded under the thorax. Red-brown.

Two similar species, one of which may be a subspecies of the other, are found in Alaskan waters. *H. mertensii* differs from *H. grebnitzkii* primarily in that it has 4 longitudinal rows of spines on the right cheliped instead of 3. *H. mertensii* ranges from the Aleutian Islands to Puget Sound, while *H. grebnitzkii* is found from the Pribilof Islands and Cape Newenham on the north side of the Bering Sea to Humboldt Bay, California. Both occur in the shallow subtidal zone. They are rarely seen out in the open but are common under rocks and logs.

157 *Placetron wosnesenskii*

Carapace length to about 7.6 centimeters (3 inches). Carapace, legs, and chelipeds have a scaly appearance. A row of spines runs along each leg. Chelipeds nearly equal in size, the right one only slightly larger than the left. Movable dactyl of each cheliped as long or longer than the stationary finger it opposes. Abdomen thin, flat, soft and not completely covered by calcareous plates. Orange-tan with brighter orange markings.

From the Aleutian Islands to Puget Sound. Subtidal to 110 meters (60 fathoms). On hard surfaces where there are crevices in which it can hide. More active at night than during the day.

158 *Acantholithodes hispidus*

Carapace length to at least 6.4 centimeters (2½ inches); width slightly less. Carapace flattened and covered with numerous short spines that have bristlelike hairs. Chelipeds and walking legs with numerous similar, but larger and stronger, spines. Abdomen short, broad, soft and with a spiny covering. Rostrum tipped by strong spines. Chelipeds unequal, the movable dactyl of each shorter than the finger it opposes. General color, yellow, suffused with brick red; fingers of claws, bright red with white teeth and black tips.

From the Aleutian Islands to central California. From the shallow subtidal zone to about 150 meters (82 fathoms) in rocky areas.

159 *Rhinolithodes wosnessenskii*

Carapace length to about 5 centimeters (2 inches); width of carapace at posterior edge slightly greater than length. Carapace is triangular in shape, with a deep, semicircular depression surrounding a large, smooth, hemispherical knob on the upper surface. Remainder of carapace covered with tubercles. Chelipeds and legs have short, stout and pointed spines with coarse, curved hairs at their tips. Gray-tan with orange markings in depression and on carapace.

From Amchitka Island in the Aleutians to northern California. Subtidal. Usually found on rock surfaces.

160 *Phyllolithodes papillosus*

Carapace length to about 7.6 centimeters (3 inches); width slightly less than length. Carapace is triangular in shape, with rounded tubercles surrounding a depressed area in the center of the dorsal surface. Large spines on lateral edges of carapace. Rostrum is prominent, with 2 prongs. Chelipeds and legs are covered with long, flattened and blunt spines. Calcareous abdominal plates have raised edges outlining a central membranous area. Tan to brown with orange markings.

From Kodiak Island and Prince William Sound to central California. Subtidal to at least 30 meters (16.4 fathoms). Usually on rock surfaces. Juveniles have short spines and a carapace that is partially or completely white.

161 *Cryptolithodes sitchensis*

Length of carapace to about 5 centimeters (2 inches); width about two-thirds greater than length. Carapace has lateral extensions concealing legs from a dorsal view. Rostrum broadest at squared tip. Abdominal plates without raised edges. Chelipeds are smooth with only a faintly rounded, longitudinal ridge below the middle of the outer surface. Variations in color and color pattern are almost limitless — may be red, olive, or orange; solid, spotted or marbled.

From Salisbury Sound, Southeastern Alaska, to central California; low intertidal and subtidal. Usually on bedrock.

162 *Cryptolithodes typicus*

Length of carapace to about 3.8 centimeters (1½ inches);

width to about two times length. Carapace has lateral extensions concealing legs from a dorsal view. Rostrum becomes narrower toward rounded tip. Abdominal plates have raised edges. Chelipeds have tubercles, including several ridges of tubercles on the outer surface. Color and color pattern extremely variable, often yellow-white to brown.

From Amchitka Island in the Aleutian Islands to central California. Low intertidal and subtidal to at least 73 meters (40 fathoms); on gravel slopes, shell debris, or rock.

163   *Lopholithodes mandtii* — Box Crab

Carapace length to about 22.8 centimeters (9 inches); width somewhat greater than length. Carapace of adults is convex, heavy and has 4 large, cone-shaped humps (anterior hump the largest). Blunt spines run along the forward edge of the carapace. Chelipeds are massive, with white teeth. Legs are short, can be folded under the carapace and have rounded, blunt, knoblike tubercles. Adults, orange-brown with bright purple markings, especially around the mouth; young specimens are brilliantly colored in scarlet, white, and purple and have an anterior hump that is proportionally larger and higher than adults have.

From Kodiak Island to central California. Shallow subtidal to 100 meters (55 fathoms) or more; on steep bedrock areas. Adults occasionally occur in groups of several females with one male. One of the largest Alaskan crabs — may weigh 10 pounds or more.

164   *Lopholithodes foraminatus* — Box Crab

Carapace length to about 15.2 centimeters (6 inches); width one-third greater than length. Carapace is heavy, covered with wartlike tubercles, and with spines at edges. Legs are covered with spiny tubercles and can be folded under carapace. A semicircular indentation is located on the outer edge of each cheliped and a similar, more shallow indentation lies on the forward edge of each of the first walking legs. When the chelipeds and legs are tucked in, a round hole, or foramen, is formed on each side of the crab by the joining of the indentations. Background, tan; spines and tubercles, red-brown.

From Kodiak Island to southern California. Subtidal at depths of 20-600 meters (11-328 fathoms). Occurs in deeper waters than does *L. mandtii*. Feeds on bivalves and organic debris. Burrows backward into sand. The two foramina probably allow incurrent water to flow to gills when the crab is partially buried.

165 *Paralithodes camtschatica* — King Crab

Carapace length to about 20.3 centimeters (8 inches); total span with outstretched legs to about 150 centimeters (59 inches). Rostrum has 4 spines — a sharp anterior spine; a second, dorsally pointed spine; and 2 lateral spines. Mid-dorsal area of carapace has 3 pairs of large spines; more spines on dorsal surface of carapace, the legs and chelipeds. Dorsal surface, dull red; underside, yellow-white.

From Norton Sound to northern British Columbia. Subtidal from about 2-250 meters (1-137 fathoms). Found in deep water during the summer. Moves to shallow water in the winter and spring to mate and molt. In the spring, a mature male will grasp a mature female, and after the latter molts, mating occurs. The female carries as many as 300,000 eggs under the rounded abdominal flap for 11.5 months. The larvae are planktonic for 2 months before settling to the sea floor. Small, long-spined juveniles may be found alone among low intertidal and shallow subtidal rocks or algae. Larger juveniles group into "pods" of many hundreds of animals and may be encountered in shallow waters. Adults occur in segregated groups or in mixed groups. The life span is 15-20 years. Adults often have leeches or leech eggs attached to their bodies. Feeds mostly on bottom-dwelling invertebrates. The young are prey to many fishes, and adults are taken by halibut and octopuses. Weighing as much as 26 pounds, *P. camtschatica* is the largest Alaskan crab species and is commercially important.

166 *Paralithodes platypus* — Blue King Crab

Carapace length to about 17.8 centimeters (7 inches). Rostrum is short with 2 large spines and several small dorsal spines. Mid-dorsal area of carapace with 2 pairs of sharp spines; more spines on dorsal surface of carapace, the chelipeds and legs. Dark olive-brown above; purple-blue on sides and legs; yellow-white on underside.

From Norton Sound to Southeastern Alaska; distribution

spotty. May be solitary or in small groups. Juveniles (without sharp spines, often with a white carapace) may be seen clinging to undersides of sunken logs or other wood debris. Adults are similar in appearance to *P. camtschatica* but differ in color and spination. Individual crabs weigh as much as 14 pounds. The species makes up a minor part of commercial king crab catch.

167　*Pagurus hirsutiusculus* — Hermit Crab

Length of carapace about 0.9 centimeter (⅜ inch). Carapace, chelipeds, and legs, hairy. Antennae, green with white spots; legs, green-black; second and third legs with white or blue-white bands at joint of dactyl and the adjacent article.

From the Pribilof and Aleutian islands to San Diego, California. Intertidal to 100 meters (55 fathoms). This is the most common small intertidal hermit crab in Southeastern Alaska. Abundant among cobble rocks and under intertidal algae. Feeds primarily on detritus.

168　*Pagurus ochotensis* — Hermit Crab

Length of carapace to about 3.8 centimeters (1½ inches). Inner surface of chelipeds marked with spines and numerous tubercles. Dorsal surface of dactyls of second and third legs marked with longitudinal rows of spines separated by two shallow grooves. Dorsal surface of "hand" of cheliped has a dark red band where it is joined by the dactyl, as well as along the cutting edge of the claw; upper parts of chelipeds usually have areas of opalescence; eyes, yellow-green.

From the Bering Sea to Oregon. Subtidal to 250 meters (137 fathoms).

169　*Elassochirus tenuimanus* — Hermit Crab

Length of carapace to about 3.2 centimeters (1¼ inches). Right chela is greatly enlarged, its dorsal surface is marked with spines or tubercles. Segment adjacent to right chela almost triangular, not expanded laterally into winglike projections. Color generally orange-brown; areas of blue on the chelipeds and walking legs; spines, white.

From the Bering Sea and Aleutian Islands to Puget Sound. Intertidal and subtidal to 224 meters (122.5 fathoms).

170 *Elassochirus cavimanus* — Hermit Crab

Length of carapace to about 3.2 centimeters (1¼ inches). Segment of right cheliped adjacent to chela flattens into winglike projections; dorsal surface has one or more irregular rows of small spines. Pincers usually dark red with cream-colored cutting edges; others segments of chelipeds, lavender-purple; walking legs, dark red with white spots.

From the Bering Sea to Puget Sound. Subtidal, usually in 35-250 meters (19-137 fathoms).

171 *Elassochirus gilli* — Hermit Crab

Length of carapace to about 3.8 centimeters (1½ inches). Segment of right cheliped adjacent to chela flattens into winglike projections; dorsal surface rounded and without spines. Bright, uniform orange-red.

From the Aleutian Islands to Puget Sound. Shallow subtidal to 65 meters (35.5 fathoms); occasionally in low intertidal zone. Often found on rock substrate. Large and conspicuous.

172 *Discorsopagurus schmitti* — Hermit Crab

Length of carapace to about 0.9 centimeter (⅜ inch). Abdomen not coiled as in most other hermit crabs. Tan with irregular spots and bands of brown-orange; tips of chelipeds, tipped with orange; large white teeth on inner edge of large chela.

From Southeastern Alaska to Puget Sound. Subtidal; almost always in detached, vacated casings of annelid tube worms.

Brachyuran Crabs

173 *Oregonia gracilis* — Decorator Crab

Carapace length including rostrum to about 7.6 centimeters (3 inches); width about one-half length. Carapace nearly triangular in shape; dorsal surface with small tubercles and hooked setae. Rostrum splits into 2 long, slender, and nearly parallel parts. Chelipeds and legs are slender, long and smooth. Tan.

From the Bering Sea to central California. Low intertidal and subtidal to about 400 meters (219 fathoms). Found on rock, sand, gravel and among algae. Often almost completely hidden by algae, sponges, hydroids and other invertebrates that it attaches to its upper surfaces. Specimen in photograph on page 45 has been brushed clean.

174   *Chorilia longipes*

Carapace length including rostrum to about 5 centimeters (2 inches); width about three-fifths length. Rostrum, about half as long as the remaining carapace, splits into 2 diverging spinelike processes; dorsal surface of carapace has tubercles and sharp spines of unequal length. Chelipeds are large, slender, somewhat flattened, and roughened by tubercles and spines; legs, slender. White to flesh color with darker, often orange, irregular banding on legs.

From Kodiak Island to southern California, at about 10-1,200 meters (5.5-656 fathoms). Often found in areas of boulders.

175   *Hyas lyratus*

Carapace length to about 10 centimeters (4 inches); width one-fourth less than length. Carapace is lyre-shaped, with tubercles and a winglike, lateral expansion behind each eye; edges of expansions are toothed. Rostrum divided into 2 flattened, blunt-tipped horns. Legs are long, slender and cylindrical. Upper surface, tan to red-gray, lighter beneath; legs are occasionally banded with stripes of red and gray.

From the Bering Sea and the Aleutian Islands to Puget Sound. Low intertidal to 700 meters (383 fathoms) or more. Found ubiquitously on gravel, sand, or mud. Often covered with algae, barnacles or hydroids. *H. coarctatus,* a similar species that occurs in the Bering Sea, has rounded, rather than toothed, edges on the expansions behind the eyes.

176   *Chionoecetes bairdi* — Tanner Crab

Length of carapace to about 15.2 centimeters (6 inches); width, somewhat greater. Carapace more or less oval, with scattered tubercles and spines. Chelipeds and legs with short spines. Legs are long, slender and flattened. Dorsal surface, light brown (pink in newly molted individuals); ventral surface, yellow-white.

From the Bering Sea to Washington; shallow subtidal to about

500 meters (273 fathoms). Usually found on soft surfaces but sometimes on bedrock or boulders in shallow water. May live for 13-14 years. Females mature at about 6 years and cease molting thereafter. A female may carry as many as 300,000 eggs under the protective abdominal flap. Young hatch in spring and are planktonic for about 2 months before settling to the sea floor. Commercially important. *C. opilio,* a similar species found in the Bering Sea, may be distinguished by a carapace that is slightly longer than wide and has fewer spines on its surface.

177 *Pugettia gracilis*

Carapace length including rostrum to about 5 centimeters (2 inches); excluding the rostrum, carapace is about as wide as long; distance between eyes equal to about one-half the greatest carapace width. Carapace is lyre-shaped to oval. The rostrum has 2 spines, and 3 large, toothlike projections are on each side of the anterior edge of the carapace. Dorsal surface of carapace with tubercles. Legs slender. Legs and dorsal surface of carapace are red-brown but carapace is occasionally totally or partially white; chelae, blue with red tips.

From the Pribilof and Aleutian islands to central California. Low intertidal to about 75 meters (41 fathoms). Found in rocky areas, often clinging to kelp or anemones. Algae and other camouflaging materials are sometimes attached to hooked setae near the base of the rostrum. *P. producta,* a similar species, reaches a length of 17 centimeters (6.7 inches), has a smooth dorsal surface on the carapace and distance between the eyes is less than about one-third the greatest carapace width.

178 *Lophopanopeus bellus*

Carapace length to about 1.9 centimeters (¾ inch); width one-half greater than the length. The carapace is hexagonal in shape. The edge between the eyes is smooth. With 3 teeth on anterior, lateral margin of carapace. Posterior edge smooth. Color variable, from red-brown to gray, and is often irregularly patterned; the fingers of chelae are dark, but the dark color does not extend back to the broad palm.

From Prince William Sound to central California. Found in low intertidal and shallow subtidal zones. Usually located in rocky areas, but often found under rocks on softer surfaces.

179   *Hemigrapsus nudus*

Carapace length to about 3.8 centimeters (1½ inches); width slightly greater than length. Outline of carapace is nearly rectangular. Posterior surface of carapace is smooth and flat; anterior surface has small, scattered granules. Legs and chelipeds are smooth. Color, variable, often dark red but may be red or purple mottled with white; chelipeds always have dark spots.

From Southeastern Alaska to Baja California. Intertidal, usually under loose rocks and in crevices. *H. oregonensis,* which occurs from Prince William Sound to Baja California, is similar in size and shape but is usually gray-green, lacks dark spots on the chelipeds, and has hair on the legs.

180   *Telmessus cheiragonus*

Carapace length to about 10 centimeters (4 inches); width of carapace about one-fourth greater than length. Carapace more or less pentagonal in shape with toothed anterior and lateral edges. Surface of carapace has large granules from which arise numerous bristles. Legs and chelipeds also with bristles. Chelipeds, short. Legs, moderately long. Yellow-brown to dark red above; yellow on lateral surfaces and undersides.

From Norton Sound to California. Low intertidal to about 40 meters (22 fathoms). Usually in areas of low kelp on bedrock, boulders, sand or shell. In Norton Sound this species often burrows in sand. Feeds on carrion and other invertebrates, such as the crab *Hyas;* may forage by digging in sand. *Erimacrus isenbeckii,* which occurs in the Bering Sea, is a similar, larger species in which the carapace is longer than it is wide.

181   *Cancer magister* — Dungeness Crab

Carapace width to about 22.8 centimeters (9 inches) or more; length about two-thirds of width. Carapace widest at 10th (last) tooth on anterior lateral edge; these last teeth are largest and set off from the rest. The leg's terminal segment is flattened. Dorsal surface, yellow-brown to gray-brown; underside, yellow-white; fingers of chelipeds are without dark color.

From the western Aleutian Islands and Cook Inlet to Baja California. Low intertidal and subtidal to about 90 meters (49 fathoms); usually found on or buried in sand. When the crab is buried, the chelipeds are held tight against the front of the carapace. Water circulating for respiration flows through a crevice between the shell and the chelipeds. Teeth on the anterior edge of the carapace strain out any large particles of sand, and finer hairs on the front underside of the carapace strain out smaller particles. Feeds on small clams, mussels, other invertebrates and carrion. Commercially important.

182   *Cancer gracilis*

Carapace width to about 9 centimeters (3½ inches); length about two-thirds of width; carapace widest at the 9th in a series of low, dull teeth on the anterior lateral edge of the carapace. Legs are slender. Dorsal surface, usually olive; fingers of chelae, without dark color; walking legs, usually purple-red.

Southeastern Alaska to Baja California. Shallow subtidal to about 100 meters (55 fathoms) on sand or gravel. Occasionally found buried. Similar to *C. magister*, but is smaller and with more slender legs.

183   *Cancer productus*

Carapace width to about 15.8 centimeters (6¼ inches); length about two-thirds of width. Anterior edge of carapace extends forward, with 5 large, nearly equal, rounded teeth between the eye notches. Color, variable, but usually dark red above, yellow-white beneath; fingers of chelae, dark. Juveniles often have a white carapace with many close-set, curving, longitudinal stripes of darker color.

From Kodiak Island to Baja California. Intertidal to about 100 meters (55 fathoms); prefers a coarse substrate.

184   *Cancer oregonensis*

Carapace width to about 3.8 centimeters (1½ inches); length slightly less. Carapace is oval and the anterior and posterior portions do not meet at a distinct angle. Carapace widest at 7th or 8th lateral marginal tooth (12-13 teeth in all on each side). Carapace may be smooth or sculptured. Color, variable, usually dark red above and lighter beneath; fingers of chelae with dark coloring reaching more than one-half the length of their outer edges.

From the Aleutian Islands to Baja California. Low intertidal to at least 366 meters (200 fathoms). Prefers tucking itself into tight-fitting holes; often found in empty shells of the large subtidal barnacle *Balanus nubilus* or in crevices on the underside of sunken logs.

Phylum: Bryozoa

The Moss Animals

Most bryozoans, or moss animals, are marine. They are characterized by a structure called the lophophore, a horseshoe-shaped, tentacle-bearing fold of the body wall that is thrust outside the animal's protective covering to collect tiny food particles. As adults, bryozoans are usually colonial and permanently attached to a surface, but their microscopic larvae are often planktonic.

Although individual bryozoans, called zooids, are small, the colonies they form may be large and conspicuous. Each zooid is encased by a calcareous or chitinous covering called a zooecium. The colony grows as new zooids bud off from existing members and add their own "houses" to the colony's mass. Each zooecium has an opening (sometimes closed off by a hinged lid, or operculum) through which the zooid extends its lophophore in order to feed. Some bryozoan colonies have specialized zooids that are equipped with bristles or pincers and that probably function to keep the colony free of plants or animals which might otherwise settle and grow on it. In form, a bryozoan colony may be a thin crust, a bushy growth or a hard mass that resembles coral. If the members of the colony have calcareous zooecia, the colony is usually opaque; the color may be white, yellow, red, orange or brown. Chitinous colonies are usually a translucent yellow-brown.

Reproduction in bryozoans may be by asexual budding, which expands the size of a colony, or sexual, which allows for the establishment of new colonies from young that drift away and settle elsewhere.

In Alaskan waters, there are many species of bryozoans. Most are subtidal, but some occur intertidally as well. Identifying individual species is usually difficult and almost inevitably involves work with a microscope. The nonspecialist, however, will enjoy examining a colony of bryozoans under a hand lens, preferably with the colony immersed in a pan of sea water so that living animals may be seen feeding.

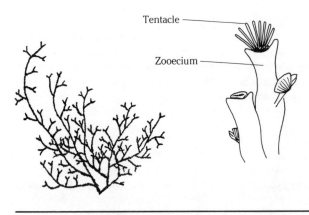

Figure 24. A bryozoan colony and an enlarged view of a group of individual zooids.

185 *Eucratea loricata*

Colony to about 10 centimeters (4 inches) in height. Branches extensively; each branch is 2 zooecia wide. Zooecia are positioned back to back in pairs along each branch. Colony, chitinous, without spines nor specialized pincerlike zooids.

Circumpolar, extending south to British Columbia. Subtidal. Superficially resembles some colonial hydroids.

186 *Membranipora* sp.

Diameter of colony to 5 centimeters (2 inches) or more. Colony flat, encrusting and often nearly circular in outline. Zooecia are usually simple in structure. Colony, white or off-white.

Species of *Membranipora* may be found throughout Alaskan waters. One species that is frequently encountered, *M. serrilamella,* occurs from Alaska to southern California. Like many other species of the genus, it may be found encrusting any appropriate surface, but it is most frequently seen on large, broad-bladed kelp.

187 *Carbasea carbasea*

Height of colony to 12 centimeters (4¾ inches). Colony is a broad, thin sheet divided into lobes. Zooids are large and arranged in a single layer in regular alternating series with all animals facing the same direction. Colony, white to light brown.

Circumpolar, from the Arctic Ocean to Prince William Sound. Subtidal to 230 meters (126 fathoms) or more. Dark brown spots, which may be seen seasonally in the colony, are soft body parts that have degenerated. The parts may be expelled after regeneration occurs.

188 *Microporina borealis*

Height of colony to 6.4 centimeters (2½ inches) or more. Colony consists of many elongate, rounded segments about 1 centimeter (0.4 inch) in length and connected to adjacent segments by chitinous joints. Colony is rigid but flexible at joints. Zooids are large and arranged in 12-16 rows around each segment; small zooids have pincers. Colony, yellow-white to tan.

Circumpolar, from the Arctic Ocean to Puget Sound. Shallow subtidal to 400 meters (219 fathoms). Found on bedrock or boulders, most frequently on vertical surfaces.

189 *Dendrobeania murrayana*

Height of colony to about 7.6 centimeters (3 inches). Forms broad, ribbonlike, blunt-tipped fronds that branch irregularly. Colony is flexible, each frond consisting of 1 layer of zooecia. Pincerlike zooids are present. Colony, light tan.

From Point Barrow to Puget Sound; shallow subtidal to about 140 meters (76.5 fathoms). Usually found on bedrock or boulders.

190 *Phidolopora pacifica*

Height of colony to about 7 centimeters (2¾ inches). Colony is upright, rigid, calcareous, lacelike and fragile. Zooids on a particular branch all face same direction. Pincerlike zooids are present. Colony, pale orange-pink.

From Southeastern Alaska to Peru. Shallow subtidal to 183

meters (100 fathoms). In Alaskan waters this species commonly lives between 15 and 30 meters (8-16 fathoms). Usually found on vertical rock surfaces.

191 *Heteropora* sp.

Height of colony to about 10 centimeters (4 inches). Colony is upright, rigid, and branching irregularly in 3 dimensions. Zooids are arranged on thick, truncate branches. Surface of colony with a slightly roughened texture.

Species of *Heteropora* occur from the Bering Sea to California. Subtidal on boulders or bedrock. Often used as a spawning substrate for some fishes, especially the buffalo sculpin. In the photograph on page 50, pink and white rays of brittle stars extend upward through the *Heteropora* colony.

192 *Flustrella* sp.

Colonies of the genus *Flustrella* are encrusting or upright and branched with flat, thick lobes. Upright forms are as much as 12 centimeters (4¾ inches) in height. Members of the genus have chitinous zooecia and numerous, flexible, chitinous spines. Yellow-brown to yellow-gray.

Species of *Flustrella* occur from the Arctic to California and may be intertidal as well as subtidal.

Phylum:
Brachiopoda

The Lamp Shells

Brachiopods have existed for more than 600 million years. Of the more than 30,000 species that existed, only about 200 species remain; only a few live in the eastern North Pacific.

Externally, brachiopods resemble clams and other molluscan bivalves. However, brachiopods have a two-part, hinged shell, and a lophophore similar to that found in bryozoans. In most cases they have a muscular stalk, called a pedicel, that attaches the animal to the substrate.

Brachiopods are divided into two classes, the Inarticulata and the Articulata. Members of the Inarticulata have valves held together by body tissues and a lophophore without skeletal support. The Articulata, the class to which the common Alaskan species belong, is comprised of brachiopods with valves held together by hinged teeth and sockets. They also have a lophophore supported by a calcareous loop attached to the lower valve.

The common Alaskan brachiopods have a shell in which the upper valve is larger than the lower. The upper valve extends beyond the lower near the hinge and has an opening through which the pedicel extends. Turned upside down, the upper valve resembles one type of oil lamp used by Greeks and Romans.

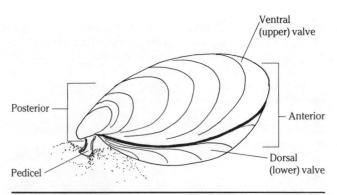

Figure 25. Brachiopod

Inside the brachiopod shell, the soft animal is oriented so the valves correlate with its dorsal and ventral sides, rather than with the left and right sides as is the case with molluscan bivalves. Occupying more than half of the internal space of the brachiopod shell is a lophophore that resembles two coiled arms with hundreds of tentacles.

Brachiopods are sessile animals. They can open their shells only so far as to form a narrow slit large enough to permit water to enter and escape. As filter feeders, they have tracts of cilia to move water past the lophophore on which food is trapped.

In most cases, brachiopods release eggs and sperm to the surrounding waters. The larvae that develop from the fertilized eggs are planktonic. In a few species, the young are brooded by the parent.

193 *Terebratalia transversa*

To 3.8 centimeters (1½ inches) from beak to opposite margin; width of shell the same or slightly greater. Shell appearance is extremely variable; may be oval to fan-shaped, smooth or with radiating ribs; anterior margin always flexed, sometimes wavy. Brick red to yellow or white.

From Mexico to Prince William Sound. Intertidal and subtidal to 1,700 meters (929 fathoms). Intertidally on the underside of large boulders; in Alaska, it is most abundant subtidally, where it is often found on vertical surfaces of large boulders or bedrock. Often heavily encrusted with other organisms. The most common brachiopod in the Pacific Northwest.

194 *Terebratulina unguicula*

To about 2.5 centimeters (1 inch) from beak to opposite margin. Shell narrow and inflated, with prominent radiating ribs that may branch. Valve edges are straight except for interlocking "saw-tooth" crenulations formed by the ends of the raised ribs. Off-white.

From southern California to Southeastern Alaska. Intertidal to 200 meters (109 fathoms) or more. Occurs intertidally in areas of broken rock and coralline algae, but in Alaskan waters it is more frequently found subtidally. Often inhabits dead bivalve and gastropod shells or interstices of old siliceous sponges. Small individuals are occasionally attached to the periostracum of the hairy triton, *Fusitriton oregonensis.*

195 *Hemithyris psittacea*

To about 2.5 centimeters (1 inch) from beak to opposite margin. Nearly triangular in shape; globose. Usually smooth with faint radiating lines but may be coarsely ribbed. In small specimens, the anterior edge of shell is straight; in older specimens, the edge is marked by a deep, broad dip. Dark gray to black.

Circumpolar, ranging from the Arctic Ocean and Aleutian Islands to Oregon. Subtidal to 400 meters (219 fathoms). Usually found on rocks.

Phylum: Phoronida

The Phoronids

Like bryozoans and brachiopods, members of the Phoronida possess a lophophore. In phoronids, this structure is typically horseshoe-shaped, bears two rows of tentacles, and curves into a spiral on both sides. Unlike brachiopods, which have an external, bivalved shell, and bryozoans, which secrete a chitinous or calcareous covering, phoronids live in soft tubes. These tubes are embedded in sand or mud or burrowed into calcareous rocks or shells. Like bryozoans, phoronids feed by extending the lophophore and collecting small food particles from the surrounding water.

The lophophore is borne at one end of a long, slender body. The opposite end of the body is bulbous and anchors the animal in its tube. Both mouth and anus are at the lophophoral end of the phoronid. The gut is a long, U-shaped structure that begins at the mouth and ends at the anus. The animal has simple nervous and circulatory systems. If the body wall is thin and translucent, blood vessels are visible.

Some phoronid species are typically a few millimeters long, while others reach lengths of 25.4 centimeters (10 inches) or more. The number of tentacles on the lophophore, the shape of the lophophore, and the nature and arrangement of muscles vary according to species.

Some species of phoronids have separate sexes; others are

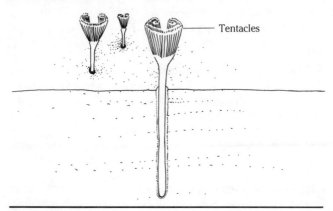

Tentacles

Figure 26. Phoronid

hermaphroditic. Certain species brood eggs and young in the lophophore. The larvae are free-swimming.

Alaskan phoronids are not well studied. At least two species are reported for British Columbia, and it is possible that these, and perhaps others, occur in Alaskan waters.

196 Phoronids

Total lengths of animals unknown; portions of animals extended from tube and above substrate about 1.9 centimeters (¾ inch); diameter of lophophores about 1.3 centimeters (½ inch). Body wall, translucent, pale orange.

The phoronids in the photo on page 51 were in sand at a depth of about 9 meters (5 fathoms). They are abundant where present and occur in groups that cover an area from a few square centimeters to a square meter or more. They respond to disturbance by retracting into their tubes.

Phylum:
Echinodermata

Crinoids, Asteroids, Ophiuroids, Echinoids and Holothuroids

Echinodermata, the phylum of "spiny-skinned" marine animals, include five classes — Crinoidea (feather stars and sea lilies), Asteroidea (sea stars), Ophiuroidea (brittle stars), Echinoidea (sea urchins and sand dollars), and Holothuroidea (sea cucumbers). Although the phylum is diverse, all echinoderms share several key characteristics.

They are radially symmetrical, many of them being divisible into five wedges, as a typical five-rayed sea star would be. Because of this radial symmetry, an echinoderm's main structures, both internal and external, radiate from near the center of the animal. In most echinoderms, it is easy to see this symmetry. Only in sea cucumbers is there some difficulty, due to the animal's elongate shape, the frequent inequality of the five sectors, and the occasional absence of tube feet (podia), which indicate the radial divisions. Sea cucumbers also have qualities of bilateral symmetry.

An echinoderm's skeleton consists of calcareous pieces called ossicles. In urchins, many ossicles are plates of varying sizes and shapes fitting together tightly to form the test, a slightly flattened, hollow sphere that is the urchin's internal skeleton. The ossicles of sea stars, brittle stars, and crinoids also form an internal skeleton. Sea cucumbers have ossicles, too, but they are usually microscopic, embedded in the skin and well separated from one another. They do not furnish the animal with any skeletal support.

The suction cup-like tube feet of echinoderms and the water-vascular system of which they are a part are unique features of this phylum. Basically, the system consists of a central, circular canal, a second canal that leads from the circular canal to the body surface, and five or more lateral canals radiating from the circular canal and bearing tube feet. Water enters this system through a porous area on the body surface. When muscles associated with the tube feet contract, water is forced out and into the canals or associated structures, creating a gripping suction at the disk-shaped tip of each tube foot. When other muscles contract, water is forced into the tube feet, their surface distends, and the suction hold is broken.

Echinoderms lack a true head region but have, instead, an oral, or mouth-bearing, surface and an opposite, aboral surface. Within the phylum, sexes are usually separate and eggs may be released to the environment or brooded.

Class Crinoidea — Feather Stars and Sea Lilies

Modern crinoids are representatives of an animal group that flourished most abundantly 350 million years ago. Remains of ancient crinoids are prominent in the fossil records of many parts of the world. Small pieces of fossilized stalks are especially familiar to geologists and paleontologists.

The main part of a crinoid, its corona, resembles a handful of feathers joined at their bases. Primitive crinoids had only five featherlike arms, but in most modern members of the group each primary arm forks one or more times creating a more complex, full crown. The coronas of some crinoids, the sea lilies, are held well above the sea floor by a long, slender stalk that persists throughout the life of the animal. In other species, the feather stars, only the young have stalks. As the individual matures, the corona breaks free from the stalk and the adult becomes mobile. In both mobile and non-mobile forms, the crinoid anchors itself to surfaces with tendril-like structures called cirri. These grow in a whorl at the base of the animal; in non-mobile species they also occur along the stalk.

Most crinoids inhabit deep water, but some species, including the one seen most frequently in Alaska, occur in shallow coastal waters. Deep-water forms are pale or white, but others are brilliantly colored.

As its form might suggest, a crinoid is a filter feeder, spreading its feathery arms into the water current to catch tiny food particles drifting by. The food is collected in a groove that extends the length of each arm and into the slender side branches that give the arm its feathery appearance. The groove is filled with mucus moved by cilia. By means of the ciliary mucous system, food is conveyed to the mouth located on the upper side of the central disk.

Feather stars and sea lilies have a water-vascular system and tube feet. The latter push food into the grooves. Neurosensory mechanisms allow the crinoid to react to touch or light changes and to right itself if overturned. Male and female crinoids simultaneously release their eggs and sperm into the sea, where fertilization takes place.

Feather Star

197 *Florometra serratissima*

Height to about 25.4 centimeters (10 inches). With 10 main arms. Slender side branches called pinnules, grade from tan at tips to reddish tan at bases.

From the Shumagin Islands to Baja California. Spotty in distribution, prefering rocky areas at depths of 10-1,000 meters (5.5-550 fathoms) or more. Adults are unstalked and walk by use of their cirri or swim off bottom by alternately unrolling and stroking with groups of arms.

Class Asteroidea — Sea Stars

There are more than 50 species of sea stars in Alaskan waters. Of these, at least a dozen commonly occur in coastal areas.

The distinctive color pattern, the number of rays, and the texture of each help identify and distinguish one species from another.

Most sea stars have between 5-24 rays. Each ray is essentially a lobe of the animal's body. Part of the digestive tract and branches of the reproductive and water-vascular systems extend into the ray. The number of rays is more or less constant within a species, and in general, the stars with the fewest rays are those for which the number is most consistent. Occasionally, however, abnormal development or an accident causes a specimen to have one or two extra or (more often) fewer rays than is typical for its species. Among species of sea stars that normally have more than five or six rays, more variability in the number is common. One of the sun stars, for example, normally has from 12-16 rays. In some species, the variation is related to age; younger animals have fewer rays, older ones more. Finally, although it is unusual, an occasional sea star may have an apparently normal ray that forks, growing a small accessory ray from its side. Such individuals are uncommon, but they demonstrate the plasticity of form among sea stars.

On the lower, or oral, surface of each ray, a sea star has rows of tube feet that extend from the center of the star to the tip of the ray. These tube feet function in locomotion over the ocean floor, catching and manipulating prey, and sensory reception. In most sea stars, the tube feet end in tiny disks that act like suction cups, enabling the animal to grip almost any solid surface. Tube feet are external parts of a water-vascular system which has its external opening in the madreporite, a smooth, porous area located slightly off-center on the aboral, or upper, surface of the sea star.

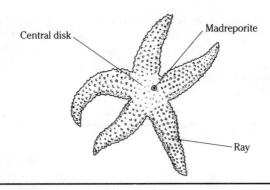

Central disk

Madreporite

Ray

Figure 27. Sea star, aboral view

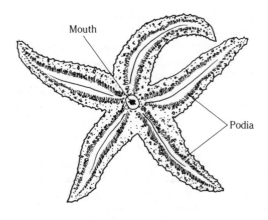

Figure 28. Sea star, oral view

Besides its rays, tube feet and madreporite, a sea star may have other distinctive external features. The upper surface and edges of the rays and disk may have spines of varying lengths or minute columnlike structures, or paxillae, that sometimes resemble geometric paving stones. Many sea stars have surface structures called pedicellariae, best seen with the aid of a magnifying glass or microscope. The pedicellariae are stalked pincers that enable the animal to clean itself and prevent organisms from settling on it. Final characteristic structures are the papulae, fingerlike projections of the star's soft skin that permit respiratory exchange of gases.

The mouth of a sea star lies at the center of its body on the lower side. Most species are carnivores and feed on living prey, although some scavenge on dead organisms to supplement their diet. A number of sea stars are particular about what they eat and will prey on only one or a few species but most will feed on a wide range of other invertebrates, such as barnacles, mussels, snails, and even other sea stars. Certain stars, if they choose to devour organisms larger than their mouths, can, by protruding the stomach, surround and digest all or part of the prey externally.

In addition to being important predators, sea stars are prey for many animals. They are eaten by crabs, including king crabs, and, where exposed by the tide, by sea gulls.

If a star is dismembered it can regenerate its missing parts. If a ray is lost, for example, it can be regrown. In some species a severed ray with a portion of the central disk intact, can develop into a complete individual.

Most species of sea stars have separate sexes and reproduce by the simultaneous release of eggs and sperm into the water. Sometimes in spring large numbers of stars aggregate in shallow water, poising on arm tips as they spawn. The larvae of these sea stars drift for a time in open water before settling to the sea floor to metamorphose to adult form. In some species, the female broods the young, cupping her body over the egg mass until the young are large enough to fend for themselves.

A number of sea stars, especially *Evasterias* and *Solaster,* serve as hosts to some scale worms. The worms, up to several centimeters in length, usually cling to the oral surface near the mouth or tuck themselves securely between adjacent rays.

Sea stars are generally most abundant in areas of boulders, cobbles, or other hard surfaces. Some species, however, have adapted to life on sandy or muddy bottoms, into which they may burrow in search of bivalves.

198 *Luidia foliolata*

Diameter to 27.9 centimeters (11 inches). With 5 long, slender, evenly tapering rays; upper surface covered with paxillae. Edges of rays with many slender, sharply pointed spines; no pedicellariae. Madreporite completely hidden by paxillae. Tube feet are large, pointed and without suction disks at tips. Body is flattened. Gray.

From Southeastern Alaska to southern California. Shallow subtidal to about 150 meters (82 fathoms) on sand or mud. Often found completely buried leaving a star-shaped depression at the surface. Inserts its tube feet into substrate to pull itself along. Known to prey on sea cucumbers and bivalves. The rays are fragile and easily broken. Uncommon in Alaska; recorded from several sites on Prince of Wales and Etolin islands.

199 *Mediaster aequalis*

Diameter to about 20.3 centimeters (8 inches). With 5 slender, tapering rays. Central disk is broad and flat. Paxillae on upper surface are edged with spines that are longer than those in the center of the paxillae. Edge of upper surface outlined with granulated plates. Upper surface, bright orange-red; lower surface, lighter salmon to flesh color.

From the Alaska Peninsula to Baja California. Subtidal to

about 275 meters (150 fathoms) on rock, sand, or mud. Feeds on sponges, bryozoans, sea pens, drift algae, and other organisms; diet varies with location and food available. May be confused with *Gephyreaster swifti,* which has a similar surface texture and coloration, but broader rays and a greater maximum size.

200 *Gephyreaster swifti*

Diameter to about 40.6 centimeters (16 inches). With 5 rays that are broad at the base and taper to blunt tips. Aboral paxillae are covered with spines of equal length, giving the paxillae a flat-topped appearance. Plates at the edge of star are distinctly separated from each other. Upper surface, orange-red to purple-red; occasional individuals may be brown.

From the Aleutian Islands to Washington. Subtidal to 350 meters (191 fathoms). Often found on sand. Known to feed on anemones, including *Metridium senile* and *Stomphia coccinea.* May be confused with *Mediaster aequalis,* a smaller sea star with somewhat different paxillae and marginal plates.

201 *Ceramaster patagonicus*

Diameter to 20.3 centimeters (8 inches). With 5 very short, rapidly tapering rays. Central disk broad with thickened edges. Upper surface covered with granular paxillae. Plates at edge of star are large, rounded and resemble beads — the largest of these are between the rays and the smallest are at the tips of the rays. Upper surface, orange-red; lower surface, off-white to flesh-colored.

From the Bering Sea to the Gulf of California. Subtidal to 240 meters (131 fathoms) or more. Several other species of *Ceramaster* occur in Alaska. Of these *C. arcticus* is the most commonly seen from Southeastern Alaska to the Aleutian Islands in shallow waters on bedrock or boulders. *C. arcticus* is smaller than *C. patagonicus,* and its upper surface may be uniform red or geometrically patterned with dark red against a lighter red or pink background.

202 *Hippasteria* sp.

Diameter to about 20.4 centimeters (8 inches). Body stout. Central disk comprises most of the star. Has 5 rays, each broad at base and tapering to a blunt tip. Upper surface has stout, blunt spines, each surrounded by a circle of granules, and with large clamlike pedicellariae embedded in the surface. Edges have slightly larger, blunt spines. Upper surface, orange-red.

Species of *Hippasteria* are not common in shallow waters but do occur from the Bering Sea to California. The most abundant species is *H. spinosa,* which is characterized by tall, slender, tapering spines on the edges and upper surface. It may feed primarily on sea pens.

203 *Dermasterias imbricata* — Leather Star

Diameter to 25.4 centimeters (10 inches). With 5 short, tapered rays. Body is stout, thick and covered with a tough, leathery membrane. No spines except along the furrows containing the tube feet. Papulae, grouped in clusters, form 6-8 irregular rows on the upper surface of each ray. Pedicellariae are usually present in the same clusters. Color, variable but usually with mottled hues of red to rust-brown and gray-green or blue. Slippery to the touch because of exuded mucus.

From Cook Inlet to central California. Low intertidal and shallow subtidal. Found on rock, sand, mud or rubble. Capable of everting its stomach, but usually ingests prey whole; may feed on anemones, sea cucumbers, sea squirts and sponges.

204 *Solaster endeca* — Sun Star

Diameter to 40.6 centimeters (16 inches). Soft-bodied. Diameter of central disk about one-third that of entire animal. With 7-13 rays, usually 9-11 among Alaskan specimens (most often 10). Paxillae on upper surface are small, crowded, almost contiguous and slightly larger near edge than at center of disk. Marginal plates are small and not obvious. Rays generally "pudgy," sometimes with a slight constriction at the base. Upper surface, red to orange or purple; underside, paler.

From Point Barrow to Washington. Intertidal and subtidal to 180 meters (98 fathoms). Found on sand or rock. Feeds primarily on sea cucumbers.

205 *Solaster stimpsoni* — Sun Star

Diameter about 30.5 centimeters (12 inches). Soft-bodied.

Long, slender rays usually number 10, occasionally 9. Central disk about one-fourth total diameter of animal. Paxillae are relatively large and appear to be more widely spaced than those of *S. endeca*. Upper surface, usually orange to pink, with a wide, gray-blue streak down the midline of each ray. Occasional specimens, solid gray-blue.

From the Bering Sea and Kodiak Island to Oregon. Found in the intertidal zone to about 60 meters (33 fathoms). Usually found on mud, cobbles or steep cliffs. Feeds primarily on small sea cucumbers. Closely related to *S. endeca* but may be distinguished by its long rays and more loosely packed, larger paxillae.

206 *Solaster dawsoni* — Sun Star

Diameter to about 40.6 centimeters (16 inches). Soft-bodied. Long, tapering rays number 8-13, commonly 11-12. Central disk about one-third total diameter of star. Paxillae are relatively large and well spaced. Marginal plates are large and distinct. Upper surface, purple gray to orange; lower surface, lighter.

From the Aleutian Islands to central California. Low intertidal to 200 meters (109 fathoms). Often found on sand-mud surfaces, cobbles or steep cliffs. Preys on other sea stars, often on *S. stimpsoni* and *Dermasterias imbricata*. Similar in appearance to *S. endeca*. Rays of *S. endeca*, though, are generally "pudgier" and lack the distinctive, larger marginal plates of *S. dawsoni*.

207 *Crossaster papposus* — Rose Star

Diameter to 20.3 centimeters (8 inches). Soft-bodied. Evenly tapering rays number 8-13, commonly 10 or 11. Stout, evenly spaced, uncrowded paxillae have as many as 50 slender spinelets each and give upper surface a rough texture. Color variable but usually red is a dominant color and pink, white, or orange may occur; markings are primarily in concentric bands.

Circumpolar, south to Oregon. Intertidal to 25 meters (13.6 fathoms) or more; usually occurs on bedrock but is also found on sand and mud. Feeds on sea pens, nudibranchs, chitons and other invertebrates. Preyed upon by the sea star *Solaster dawsoni*.

208   *Pteraster tesselatus*

Diameter to 17.8 centimeters (7 inches) or more. Body stout, inflated and cushionlike; thickness equal to about one-third diameter. Five rays, broad at base, are short and thick; with straight or swollen sides, and blunt, upturned tips. Upper surface, covered with a thick, spongy membrane, has mosaic-like appearance. Paxillae with 18-21 spinelets (as a rule these do not protrude through surface membrane). Upper surface has a conspicuous, slightly elevated central opening that leads to a spongy cavity between the body wall and the external membrane. Madreporite not evident. Upper surface, yellow-brown to pale orange, often mottled.

From the Bering Sea to Washington. Subtidal, 10-400 meters (5.5-219 fathoms) or more; usually found on bedrock or among boulders. Secretes copious quantities of mucus. Its diet is varied, but sponges probably are an important food.

209   *Pteraster militaris*

Diameter to 15.2 centimeters (6 inches) or more. Body thick, stout, soft. With 5 rays. Upper surface covered with a thick, wrinkled membrane that completely obscures spine-bearing paxillae lying beneath the exterior surface. Upper surface with a conspicuous, slightly elevated central opening that leads to a spongy cavity between the body wall and the external membrane. Madreporite not evident. Yellow or yellow-red to pink.

Circumpolar, south to Washington. Subtidal, 10-1,000 meters (5.5-550 fathoms). Usually found on mud. Similar to *P. tesselatus,* but has relatively larger rays.

210   *Henricia leviuscula* — Blood Star

Diameter to 15.2 centimeters (6 inches) or more. With 5 long, slender rays that appear almost straight rather than tapered. Paxillae are moderately large and close-set. Marginal plates are squarish and large, but not separated by prominent grooves. Upper surface, often bright red-orange but may also be tan, purple, or mottled; lower surface, paler.

From the Aleutian Islands to southern California. Intertidal to 100 meters (55 fathoms) or more. Usually found on bedrock. Females brood eggs, often hiding under or between rocks. Feeds primarily on encrusting sponges; may feed on plankton by positioning itself in a current and extending one or more rays into the water. May be confused with *H. sanguinolenta.*

211 *Henricia sanguinolenta*

Diameter to 15.2 centimeters (6 inches) or more. With 5 long, slender rays that are moderately thick at the base and tapered. Paxillae with spines on upper surface. Marginal plates are inconspicuous. Color, variable — often mottled or with two-tone coloration.

Circumpolar, south to Washington. Shallow subtidal to perhaps 300 meters (164 fathoms) or more. Females brood their eggs. Similar in appearance to *H. leviuscula* with which it may intergrade. *H. sanguinolenta* is generally heavier bodied and has rays that are somewhat thicker at the base than those of *H. leviuscula.* In addition, its paxillae are smaller and marginal plates less conspicuous.

212 *Lethasterias nanimensis*

Diameter to 61 centimeters (24 inches) or more. With 5 long, slender, flexible rays. Large spines on upper surface are each surrounded by a dense wreath of crossed pedicellariae. Background color on upper surface, yellow-brown; spines tipped with black.

From the Aleutian Islands to Washington. Shallow subtidal to about 100 meters (55 fathoms). Found on mud, sand, gravel and boulders. It superficially looks like *Orthasterias koehleri* in shape and spination, but may be distinguished by the different coloration.

213 *Orthasterias koehleri*

Diameter to 40.6 centimeters (16 inches) or more. With 5 long, slender, flexible rays. Spines on upper surface of each ray are arranged in 5 or more rows. Most pedicellariae are concentrated in clusters around a central spine. Spines on upper surface, pink. General coloration of pink-red to dark red in bands against a light background.

From the eastern Aleutian Islands to Prince William Sound to central California. Low intertidal to 230 meters (126 fathoms) but most often subtidally in Alaska on a variety of surfaces, including bedrock, boulder and sand-shell. May feed on a variety of organisms, but apparently prefers the bivalve *Humilaria kennerleyi.*

214 *Leptasterias hexactis*

Diameter to 9 centimeters (3½ inches). With 6 rays, each broad at base and evenly tapered to blunt tip. A few, irregularly placed spines on upper surface. With pedicellariae. Usually drab gray, gray-green, or nearly black, but sometimes with yellow to greenish white markings; occasionally an orange or red specimen is found.

From the Shumagin Islands and Kodiak Island to central California. Common among loose cobbles and on bedrock of the lower intertidal area, but less abundant in shallow subtidal waters. In winter and early spring individuals congregate under rocks to spawn. Females brood their eggs, clinging tightly to rocks to protect the egg clusters hidden beneath their bodies. Brooding lasts about 60 days until young are about 1 millimeter (0.04 inch) in diameter. *L. hexactis* feeds on barnacles, small sea cucumbers, chitons, limpets and snails. The taxonomy of this creature is unsettled; a number of forms of the species have been described. Numerous other species of *Leptasterias* have been reported from Alaskan waters, many of them in the Kodiak Island, Aleutian Islands and Bering Sea regions. Many, but not all, members of this genus have 6 rays.

215 *Evasterias troschelii*

Diameter usually to about 30.5 centimeters (12 inches); occasional subtidal specimens may be 60 centimeters (23½ inches) in diameter. With 5 slender, tapered rays. Pedicellariae are scattered on the upper surface. Upper surface with spines that may or may not be uniform in size and that may or may not be arranged in an obvious pattern. Commonly gray-green, but may be any of many shades of brown, green, orange, or purple.

From the Pribilof Islands to central California. Intertidal down to 10 meters (5.5 fathoms) or more. Found on bedrock, cobbles, or sand. Feeds on barnacles, sea squirts, bivalves and other invertebrates. May be confused with *Pisaster ochraceus,* but *E. troschelii* has proportionately longer, more slender rays and a less pronounced network of spines on the upper surface. Its color phases only occasionally include the deep purple col-

oration of many specimens of *P. ochraceus*. Like *P. ochraceus,*
E. troschelii often forms dense aggregations.

216 *Pisaster ochraceus*

Diameter to about 30.5 centimeters (12 inches). Body is thick,
firm and stiff. With 5 fat rays. Upper surface has numerous,
blunt, stout, white spines arranged in an irregular network.
Pedicellariae of several kinds are clustered or scattered
among papulae. Occurs in two main color phases, purple and
orange-ochre; some specimens are brown.

From Baja California to Prince William Sound. Usually intertidal and prominently visible at low tide, often in clusters of
several to many individuals. Most frequently found in areas of
wave action or current. May be one of the most obvious and
abundant sea stars in areas where it occurs. Feeds on
barnacles, bivalves, limpets, snails, chitons, and other
invertebrates.

217 *Pycnopodia helianthoides* —
Sunflower Star

Diameter to 1 meter (39 inches), commonly to 50.8 centimeters (20 inches). Usually begins life with 6 rays; with age,
more rays develop until mature animals have from 20-24.
Upper surface soft, with numerous, irregularly and closely
spaced groups of slender papulae. Pedicellariae clustered in
crowded groups, usually around a central white spine; other
pedicellariae scattered. Color, variable, but generally mottled
and including colors from orange to blue-gray.

From the eastern Aleutian Islands to southern California.
Intertidal to about 50 meters (27 fathoms). Found on sand,
mud or rock. One of the largest sea stars in the world. Fragile,
the rays may be easily severed. Notable for its speed and
agility, capable of traveling as much as 45.7 centimeters (18
inches) per minute. Responds quickly to the scent of food in
the water. Can readily squeeze through relatively small
openings — mature specimens often enter shrimp pots
through openings less than 6.4 centimeters (2½ inches)
diameter. Often digs bivalves for food, leaving characteristic
holes in sandy areas; also feeds on urchins, other invertebrates and dead fish. Causes a strong escape response in sea
cucumbers, scallops, abalone, cockles, some nudibranchs, and
other invertebrates. Serves as food for king crabs.

Class Ophiuroidea — Brittle Stars

Ophiuroids (brittle stars) and asteroids (sea stars) have the same body shape, but ophiuroids are distinctive in several respects. Their rays are usually longer and more slender than those of sea stars. The round or pentagonal central disk is set off from the rays, and the digestive and reproductive organs in the central disk do not extend into the rays. Unlike sea stars, which rely almost entirely on their tube feet for locomotion, brittle stars move by a sinuous flexing of their rays; their tube feet are small and more important for feeding, respiration, and sensory reception than for locomotion.

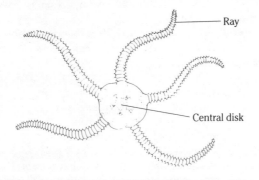

Ray

Central disk

Figure 29. Brittle star, aboral view

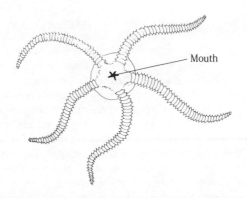

Mouth

Figure 30. Brittle star, oral view

Most brittle stars have great regenerative powers and can replace missing parts. Often brittle stars have rays marked by abrupt color changes, places where the rays were broken off and new growth began. Some brittle stars can throw off the upper, or aboral, cap of the central disk and regenerate it, too.

Although numerous both in number of species and of individuals, brittle stars may go unobserved, because they are often nocturnal and live primarily under rocks, among algae, or nestled with other invertebrates. Some are intertidal, but the majority prefer deeper waters. Some species occur only below depths of 1,000 meters (547 fathoms).

Many brittle stars scavenge or feed on organic debris, using their tube feet to convey food particles from the rays to the mouth in the center of the underside of the central disk. Some brittle stars browse on large algae or feed on bryozoans and hydroids that grow on algae. Still others, including the multiple-branching basket star, feed by stretching their rays perpendicularly to the current and straining food from the passing waters.

In most species, the sexes are separate and eggs and sperm are discharged into the water — often from large groups formed as spawning time nears. In other species, eggs are retained within brood pouches where the young develop until they appear like miniatures of their parents.

218   *Ophiura sarsii*

Diameter of disk to about 1.9 centimeters (¾ inch). Disc notch for each ray is deep and bordered on each side by a "comb" of numerous short fleshy projections distinctly separate from each other. The large aboral plates, central and adjacent to the arm combs, are elongate and triangular. With 3 spines on each side of each ray joint, upper spines being up to 2 times longer than the joint from which they arise. Color, variable, but most commonly gray, sometimes with lighter markings.

Circumpolar, as far south as Washington. Subtidal in 3-3,000 meters (1.6-1,640 fathoms). Most often seen in great numbers on sand-shell bottoms at depths greater than 15 meters (8 fathoms). It usually lies totally exposed, but occasionally is partly buried. May respond to disturbance by "leaping" along the bottom in short, rapid hops.

219   *Ophiopholis aculeata*

Diameter of central disk to about 1.9 centimeters (¾ inch).

Main plates on upper surface of rays are separated from each other by smaller plates. Color, variable, usually with some red or red-purple in streaks or blotches; may imitate surface color on which it is found.

Circumpolar, from Point Barrow to central California. Low intertidal to 2,000 meters (1,094 fathoms). The species tolerates a wide range of water temperatures and bottom types and often lives in communities with various sponges, bryozoans and encrusting coralline algae.

220   *Gorgonocephalus eucnemis* — Basket Star

Diameter of central disk to about 10 centimeters (4 inches), but usually about 5 centimeters (2 inches); total diameter to about 45.7 centimeters (18 inches). With 5 basic rays, but during development each ray divides in two at the tip, then each fork splits repeatedly to form a network of "tendrils." Usually tan or flesh-colored; may have brown mottlings on upper surface of central disk.

From Norton Sound and the Aleutian Islands to California. Shallow subtidal to deep waters. Occasionally, specimens are washed ashore. Feeds by extending rays into the water column and collecting bits of food on its outstretched tendrils. When feeding, the flat plane of the outstretched portion of the star is perpendicular to the current to strain a maximum amount of water.

Class Echinoidea — Sea Urchins, Sand Dollars and Heart Urchins

Three kinds of echinoids are found in Alaskan waters. Of these, sea urchins are the most numerous and likely to be seen. Sand dollars are locally abundant throughout Alaska's exposed coastal waters, but because they are burrowers and usually subtidal, they are not often found except by dredging. Heart urchins also burrow and are usually found in northern waters at depths of 100 meters (55 fathoms) or more.

All echinoids have a firm, internal shell called a test. This shell may be flattened, as in sand dollars, or more or less globular, as in the urchins. From the test project spines, pedicellariae, and podia. The spines of sand dollars and heart urchins are shorter than those of sea urchins.

Echinoids basically have radial symmetry, but heart urchins, which have a deep furrow that contributes to their heart-shaped appearance, and sand dollars also tend toward secondary bilateral symmetry. The mouth of most echinoids is at or near the center of the lower surface and is equipped with five sharp teeth. Deceptively delicate in appearance, the teeth and their complex jaws can bite tough materials, such as calcareous algae or plastics.

Several species of sea urchins are common in the shallow

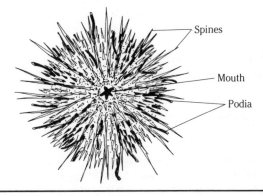

Spines

Mouth

Podia

Figure 31. Sea urchin, oral view

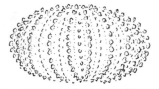

Figure 32. Sea urchin test, lateral view

marine waters of Alaska. Their fragile tests are often washed ashore, clean and in good condition. An examination of a test can tell a great deal about the animal from which it came.

The test of a sea urchin consists of many small plates. The examination of the arrangement of plates, their tubercles and pores show that bands extend from the center of the lower surface to the center of the upper surface, dividing the test into sections. Each tubercle is the base with which one of the urchin's spines articulates, and each pore is an opening through which the external tube feet are linked to the internal portion of the urchin's water-vascular system. If the central plates on the urchin's upper, or aboral, surface are intact, one may see the anal opening in the center of the plate group, the single madreporite lying to one side and, on each of five plates forming the periphery of the central area, a tiny pore through which the eggs or sperm of the urchin are extruded. The complex calcareous parts of the urchin's mouth occasionally remain intact on a beach-collected test.

The test protects the living urchin's internal organs and is itself covered by a thin skin. Projecting spines of varying length also protect the urchin and may act as levers for locomotion. Pedicellariae, usually with three jaws rather than the two of sea stars, are small, inconspicuous, and hidden among the spines. Tube feet are more obvious, often extending beyond the tips of the spines. The tube feet have suction cup tips for locomotion and moving food toward the mouth.

The shallow-water urchins of Alaska may be found in great abundance. Moving over rock or sand, these animals primarily forage on algae, but they will scavenge on animal material as well. In spite of their spiny armor, urchins fall prey to some sea stars, crabs, fishes, sea otters, river otters, ducks, sea gulls and other birds that feed along beaches.

In urchins, sexes are separate, and the animals release their eggs or sperm directly into sea water. Mature individuals have five large gonads. Those of the male are white, while the female's are orange or deep yellow. Although urchins are seldom used as food in the United States, in Europe, Asia and South America, urchin gonads are a delicacy. Gonads of common Alaska species are edible and historically were an important part in the diet of early Aleuts.

Sea Urchins

221 *Strongylocentrotus droebachiensis* — Green Urchin

Diameter of test to about 8.2 centimeters (3¼ inches). Spines of moderate size; primary spines only slightly longer and thicker than secondary spines. Spines, usually a uniform pale green; tube feet, darker than spines, usually brown to purple; occasional specimens, white or purple.

Circumpolar, south to Washington. Intertidal and subtidal to at least 130 meters (71 fathoms), especially abundant from low intertidal to about 12 meters (6.5 fathoms). Occurs on almost any surface, and is often found in dense groups. Capable of moving through an area and eating most of the plant material; feeds on large algae, diatoms and coralline algae scraped from rocks; may also feed on other urchins, jellyfish, or dead fish, and will gnaw on synthetic substances. Preyed upon by the sea star *Pycnopodia helianthoides*, king crabs, anemones, land and sea otters, eiders, sea gulls, ravens and crows. Spawns during early spring. It is the most common and widespread Alaskan urchin.

222 *Strongylocentrotus pallidus*

Diameter of test to about 6.4 centimeters (2½ inches). Spines, white, usually tinged with pink or orange but occasionally with green; coloration deepest on spines near the center of the upper surface; tube feet, usually about the same color as the spines, rarely darker.

From the Arctic Ocean to Oregon. Subtidal, below 20 meters (11 fathoms) and usually at depths of 50 meters (27 fathoms) or greater. Found on bedrock, clay, gravel, or broken shell. May burrow into soft bottoms. Very similar in appearance to white specimens of *S. droebachiensis,* but the latter does not usually burrow and generally reaches a greater size.

223 *Strongylocentrotus franciscanus* —
Red Urchin

Diameter of test to about 17.1 centimeters (6¾ inches). Spines heavy and long, to about 7 centimeters (2¾ inches) on large specimens. Spines, red-orange to maroon; tube feet, usually a deeper shade of red.

From Kodiak Island to Baja California. Occurs on the open coast and shores of major straits. Low intertidal to about 125 meters (68 fathoms), but most abundant at shallow depths of about 5-10 meters (2.7-5.5 fathoms). Usually found on rock in zones of brown algae where current or wave surge is moderate. Feeds on kelp, other algae and occasionally scavenges on dead animals. A preferred food of sea otters. Usually spawns in winter or early spring. Larvae are planktonic for about 2 months before settling to the sea floor. Juveniles may be found in the same area as adults but are hidden in crevices, among kelp holdfasts, or under adults. *S. franciscanus* is the largest of the Alaskan urchins.

224   *Strongylocentrotus purpuratus* —
Purple Urchin

Diameter of test about 9 centimeters (3½ inches); spines to 2.5 centimeters (1 inch) on mature specimens. Prevailing color of live animal, purple; immature specimens may be greenish.

From Cook Inlet to Baja California. Intertidal to about 65 meters (36 fathoms). On rock substrate. Very common in California but less so in Alaska. Usually restricted to shores with heavy wave action or strong current. Commonly lives in crevices or holes, and is capable of slowly hollowing depressions in rock with its teeth and spines. (May hollow out a hole for itself and continue to enlarge the hole as it grows, occasionally leaving the opening too small and trapping itself inside the rock.) Intertidal populations tend to remain in one restricted area, feeding on algae in the immediate vicinity and waiting for drift algae brought by waves or currents. Spawns in winter, at least in its more southerly range.

Sand Dollar

225   *Dendraster excentricus*

Diameter of test to about 8.2 centimeters (3¼ inches). Test flattened, nearly circular in outline. Spines are short, numerous and give a velvety appearance to the surface of the live animal. Madreporite located off-center on upper side; the 5 areas where tube feet radiate from the madreporite are indicated by a starlike pattern on the test; additional tube feet occur on both upper and lower surfaces. Live animal, gray to dark red or purple; test, white.

From Baja California to at least Southeastern Alaska. Usually subtidal, to at least 12 meters (6.5 fathoms) in Alaskan waters. Lives in sandy areas along the open coast and is often buried. Feeds on detritus. Eggs and sperm are released to open water and larvae are planktonic. Another species of sand dollar, *Echinarachnius parma,* which is circumpolar in distribution and may occur as far south as Puget Sound, has a more centered and symmetrical star-shaped pattern on the upper surface of the test.

Class Holothuroidea — Sea Cucumbers

Sea cucumbers are elongate animals with shapes resembling that of their namesake. In length, they range from a few centimeters to as much as 50.8 centimeters (20 inches). They may be brilliant red, dull gray or black, or they may be whitish and translucent. Their often soft, almost wormlike appearance belies the fact that they are echinoderms — close relatives of sea stars and the other "spiny-skinned" animals.

Like other echinoderms, sea cucumbers have a water-vascular system and radial symmetry, although the latter is somewhat obscured by a tendency toward bilateral symmetry. The tube feet of the water-vascular system may occur randomly on the surface of the sea cucumber, arranged in five longitudinal series which make the radial symmetry more apparent, or exist just around the anus. In many species, the tube feet on the upper side of the body have been modified, leaving only the tube feet on the underside of the animal to function in locomotion.

Beneath the outer skin of the sea cucumber are two layers of muscles — one longitudinal, the other circular. Using these muscles, the sea cucumber moves over, or burrows into the sea floor. The tube feet aid in locomotion by attaching to the surface when the cucumber is elongated, releasing their grip as the animal contracts, then attaching again when it lengthens.

The mouth of a typical sea cucumber may be surrounded with elaborate oral tentacles. With these, the animal collects food from passing water currents, mops it up from the sea floor, or sweeps it from the walls of its burrow. The oral tentacles of a feeding sea cucumber are constantly in motion, folding into the mouth with the material they have collected, then extending again to gather more.

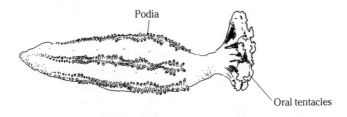

Podia

Oral tentacles

Figure 33. Sea cucumber

Sea cucumbers have a wide variety of living habits. Some burrow into sand and mud bottoms, leaving only feeding tentacles exposed. Others wedge themselves securely into clefts and crevices in bedrock or among boulders. Still others freely roam along the bottom and are capable of an erratic half-swimming, half-hopping motion when threatened by a predator.

Male and female cucumbers usually release their sperm or ova through a pore on the dorsal surface behind the mouth. In many species, the larvae that develop from the fertilized eggs are planktonic. In other species, however, the young are brooded by the female and set free only after they have assumed adult form.

Most sea cucumbers are soft, sluggish animals that would appear to be easy prey for any number of predators. Many species, however, produce a poison, holothurin, which they release into the water. If the poison enters the gills, and thus the blood stream, of a fish or other would-be predator, it can cause hemorrhaging and destruction of blood cells. A number of species of sea cucumbers apparently also use evisceration as a means of defense, expelling from the body many of their internal organs if sufficiently disturbed. Most sea cucumbers have considerable powers of regeneration and are able to regrow expelled internal organs and missing body parts in short order.

Long a food held in high esteem by Asiatic people, some sea cucumbers yield a variety of food products. Whole, eviscerated cucumbers are cooked and dried to produce trepang, or *beche de mer*. The intestines are cleaned, salted and fermented, and the gonads are dried. The longitudinal muscles are boiled or fried.

226 *Cucumaria miniata*

Length to about 20.3 centimeters (8 inches). Body cylindrical. Possesses large tube feet in 5 equally spaced, longitudinal bands. With 10 highly branched, oral tentacles. Usually orange or brown.

From Prince William Sound to central California. Low intertidal and at least shallow subtidal. Usually found among boulders or rock rubble. Most of the body is hidden, leaving oral tentacles exposed to the water current. Feeds by collecting small particles from the water on the tentacles, then cleaning the tentacles in the mouth to remove the food. Larvae are planktonic.

227   *Cucumaria vegae*

Length to about 3.8 centimeters (1½ inches). Body is short, stout and tapers to each extremity. With 3 longitudinal bands of tube feet on the lower surface and 2 reduced bands on the upper surface. With 10 oral tentacles. Body and tentacles, dark brown to black.

From the Aleutian Islands to British Columbia. Low intertidal on cobbles or bedrock. Usually found on undersides of rocks. Probably feeds on organic debris. Females brood young. Sometimes called a "tar-spot" cucumber.

228   *Parastichopus californicus*

Length to about 50.8 centimeters (20 inches). Upper surface of body has large, fleshy, pointed papillae. Lower surface has 3 longitudinal bands of tube feet. With 20 small oral tentacles. Mottled, usually reds and browns against a yellowish background.

From Prince William Sound to Mexico. Intertidal to about 200 meters (109 fathoms). Mobile on mud, sand, bedrock and shallow beds of low kelp. Feeds on organic debris by sweeping substrate with mucus-covered tentacles. May routinely eviscerate every autumn, taking 1-3 months to regenerate functional intestines. Spawns in summer, probably in shallow water; when spawning, the animal's anterior end is raised off the bottom and a fine stream of eggs or sperm is extruded through a pore on the dorsal surface. Larvae are planktonic. Adults have well-developed powers of locomotion, will swim weakly if contacted by predatory sea stars, such as *Pycnopodia helianthoides*. *P. californicus* is non-toxic and edible.

229   *Eupentacta quinquesemita*

Length to about 15.2 centimeters (6 inches). Body is slender, elongate and tapers to both ends with many long, stout tube feet in 5 longitudinal double bands. Has 10 feeding tentacles. Body wall, tough. Usually cream-colored but may be white to pale orange.

From at least Southeastern Alaska to California. Intertidal and subtidal in rocky areas. Feeds by filtering food particles with outstretched oral tentacles. A similar species, *E. pseudoquin-quesemita,* which has a thin body wall, more tube feet and broad areas between the bands of tube feet, grows to only about 10 centimeters (4 inches) in length and is often covered with bits of shell or other material. *E. pseudoquinquesemita* occurs from the Aleutian Islands to Puget Sound.

230 ? *Chiridota* sp.

Length to about 10 centimeters (4 inches) or more. Body is long and slender, without tube feet but with either 1 or 3 longitudinal series of ossicles on its upper surface. Usually with 12 oral tentacles. Translucent white to light pink.

Occurs at least in Southeastern Alaska and British Columbia. Subtidal. Burrows in soft sand-mud surfaces from which it extends the anterior end and feeding tentacles.

231 *Psolus chitonoides*

Length to 8.2 centimeters (3¼ inches); width about one-third length. Lower surface flattened like a foot, with a thick skin and 3 double rows of tube feet. Upper surface covered with hard, visible, calcareous plates. Oral tentacles branch, often extending upward at a 90-degree angle to the body. Tentacles, red; body, orange to orange-brown; deep-water specimens may be white.

From the Pribilof Islands to California. Low intertidal and subtidal to at least 100 meters (55 fathoms). Attaches itself firmly to exposed rocks. Feeds on microscopic organisms strained from water currents by oral tentacles.

Phylum: Chordata

The Thaliaceans, Ascidians and Their Allies

In general, chordates share three characteristics. First, they have a nerve cord, part of which is enlarged into a brain, on the dorsal side of the body. Second, a notochord, a rodlike structure located beneath the nerve cord, usually appears at some stage of development. And finally, gill slits connecting the pharynx with the outside body are evident in many chordates, at least during early stages of development.

The chordates most familiar to us are members of the Vertebrata — the animals with backbones. Another group, the Urochordata, includes animals that have a notochord at some stage in their lives but possess no backbone. The urochordates are usually grouped with the invertebrates rather than the vertebrates, but they are, in a sense, a link between these two major divisions of the animal kingdom.

In Alaskan waters, urochordates are represented by members of three groups. Larvaceans (Larvacea) are small, free-swimming animals that are usually no more than a centimeter in length. Larvaceans are usually seen only when collections of minute planktonic organisms are examined. The transparent animals called salps (Thaliacea) are also free-swimming but may be much larger and more conspicuous than the larvaceans from which they also differ in shape and structure. The larger salps may be seasonally abundant and conspicuous in surface waters along the outer coast of Alaska. Ascidians (Ascidiacea) are pelagic as larvae, but as adults they become permanently attached to surfaces. Adult ascidians may be large and form a conspicuous part of bottom-dwelling marine communities.

Urochordates are sometimes called tunicates because they possess an external covering, or tunic. The tunic of larvaceans and salps is transparent; ascidian tunics may be transparent, translucent or opaque. Among ascidians, the tunic differs in color, texture, and shape which often helps in distinguishing one kind of ascidian from another.

Class Thaliacea — Salps

Members of the Thaliacea are free-swimming, transparent, barrel-shaped animals usually found near the water's surface in the open ocean. Of the three subgroups only the salps (Salpidae) are frequently seen in Alaskan waters.

Salps have a cylindrical body with an opening at each end. By contracting circular bands of muscles, a salp forces water out the posterior opening to propel itself through the water. By straining the water passing through its gill slits, the animal gathers food. Because a salp is transparent, internal structures are visible through the outer tunic; most evident are the visceral organs, which may be colored and are often visible near the posterior end of the animal.

The reproductive cycles of thaliaceans involve an alternation of generations. Typically, a solitary, asexual form of the animal produces buds that develop into one or more kinds of offspring, none of which are identical to the parent. Some or all of the offspring produced by the asexual animals reproduce sexually to give rise to another generation of solitary, asexual individuals.

232 *Salpa fusiformis*

With 2 different generations in the life history. Individuals of both generations transparent, free-swimming, with an opening at each end. Individuals of the solitary generation generally cylindrical, to about 17.8 centimeters (7 inches) in length; members of the aggregate generation generally spindle-shaped, with an elongate process at each end, to about 13 centimeters (5 inches) in length.

Widespread, from the Gulf of Alaska to California. Occur in open or coastal waters. Occasionally encountered in abundance, sometimes clogging nets and fouling other fishing gear. The asexual generation produces a chain of sexual individuals. These offspring may remain attached to the parent for a period before individuals or a series of offspring stretching 1 meter (39 inches) in length break away. Photo on page 61 is of part of a chain and includes 8 individuals. When *Salpa fusiformis* is abundant, both the solitary and aggregate generations occur in large numbers.

Class Ascidiacea — Sea Squirts

As larvae, ascidians are free-swimming, look somewhat like tadpoles, and have a notochord in the tail region. After a brief period in open water, the larvae settle to the bottom of the sea and metamorphose into adults. During this process, the tail is resorbed and the notochord disappears. The sedentary adult ascidian has little resemblance to the larva from which it developed. Adults, which live permanently attached to a solid surface, may be encrusting and superficially spongelike in appearance, or upright and shaped like barrels, clubs, or irregular lumps.

Ascidians are often called sea squirts, a name derived from the action of a disturbed ascidian, which will quickly contract its body-wall muscles and squirt a jet of water from one of its two siphons. The two siphons, characteristic of ascidians, function in respiration and feeding. When the animal is undisturbed, water moves steadily through the incurrent siphon into an internal chamber where gases are exchanged and tiny food particles from the water are caught on strands of mucus that move continuously toward the stomach. Water then passes out the ascidian through the excurrent siphon.

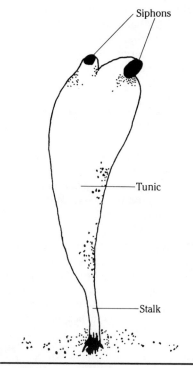

Figure 34. Ascidian

There are three general types of ascidians — solitary, social, and compound. Solitary ascidians may occur isolated or in clusters, but if clustered, each animal is separate from its neighbors. Social ascidians may, at first glance, look like clusters of solitary animals, but they have, or have had, rootlike structures, or stolons, connecting individuals. (Stolons are a part of asexual reproduction, new individuals growing out from them. In time, stolons connecting parent and offspring may degenerate, severing the visible connection between the two.) In compound ascidians, many individual animals, or zooids, share a common tunic; each member of the colony has its own incurrent opening, but may share its excurrent opening with several other members. Solitary and social ascidians are usually tall and upright or shaped like spheres. Colonial ascidians may have one of these shapes, too, but may also form thick masses or thin sheets that grow free-form over a firm surface. Social and compound ascidians commonly are capable of reproducing both sexually and asexually, but solitary ascidians reproduce only sexually.

Ascidians are generally subtidal animals and may be found from depths of a few to many meters. They require a firm surface for attachment and can only survive in waters sufficiently rich in oxygen and food material. These sedentary filter feeders probably have few enemies, but some species are known to be prey for sea stars.

233 *Ascidia paratropa*
Solitary. Height to about 15.2 centimeters (6 inches); diameter somewhat less than one-half height. Siphons, located at anterior end, are unequal; excurrent siphon taller and capable of being retracted. Surface covered by scattered, prominent tubercles. Tunic, translucent and colorless.

From California to Southeastern Alaska. Subtidal, usually at depths of 20-100 meters (11-55 fathoms) in Alaskan waters. Another species of *Ascidia, A. callosa,* is irregularly hemispherical, transparent to opaque, and usually a dirty off-white. It is often covered with detritus or other fine material and is no more than 3.2 centimeters (1¼ inches) in diameter. *A. callosa* is circumpolar and may be found in shallow subtidal waters as far south as Puget Sound.

234 *Corella willmeriana*
Solitary. Height to about 5 centimeters (2 inches); width somewhat less than height. Siphons borne on short tubes. Lower end narrowed into a short stalk by which the animal is attached to the substrate. Tunic is transparent, smooth, thin, usually colorless but may have a tinge of yellow or pink.

From Prince William Sound to Puget Sound. Subtidal to about 50 meters (27 fathoms). Usually found on hard surfaces in quiet areas of low currents; may occur on floats and pilings.

235   *Halocynthia aurantium* — Sea Peach

Solitary. Height to at least 15.2 centimeters (6 inches). Body irregularly barrel-shaped with 2 short, stout siphons at anterior end. Tunic thin but tough and leathery. Surface smooth but granular because of minute, short, stiff spines that are distributed in small groups. Red or orange, grading into yellow.

From the Chukchi Sea to Puget Sound. Subtidal to about 100 meters (55 fathoms). Often found with shrimp, usually Hippolytidae, perched on them. Preyed upon by the sea star *Evasterias troschelii.*

236   *Styela* sp.

Solitary. Height to 15.2 centimeters (6 inches) or more. Large specimens have a flexible, tough stalk that may comprise more than one-half the total length of the animal. In young specimens, the stalk may be absent or very short. Siphon openings on short tubes at anterior end of body. Red-orange, blending to yellow toward base.

Species of *Styela* occur in Alaskan waters from the Arctic and the Aleutian Islands to Southeastern Alaska. Some species, such as that in the photo on page 63, are stalked, but others, even when mature, are not. Low intertidal and subtidal. May be locally abundant.

237   *Boltenia villosa*

Solitary. Height to about 3.8 centimeters (1½ inches). Round to oblong and attached to substrate by a stalk that may be 4 times the length of the body. Siphons short, conical. Surface, including stalk, covered with spines that are short, slender to coarse, and often branched. Red-orange; color most visible at siphon apertures.

From Prince William Sound to southern California. Found in low intertidal and subtidal zones. Occurs on rocky surfaces and is often covered with organic debris and other material that adheres to its spines. *B. ovifera,* which occurs in the Arctic Ocean and Bering Sea, is similar, but its surface is either smooth or has soft, flexible spines without lateral branches. *B. echinata,* reported from the Arctic to British Columbia, may be distinguished from *B. villosa* by spines with multiple branches at the tips.

238 *Cnemidocarpa finmarkiensis*

Solitary. Height to 2.5 centimeters (1 inch); wider than high. Dome-shaped, attaches to surfaces by a broad base. Siphons situated on short tubes on anterior surface. Tunic is thin, smooth, tough and without wrinkles. Pink-orange.

Circumpolar, south to Puget Sound. Low intertidal to 500 meters (273 fathoms). Occurs on rock or other hard surfaces. Occasionally found almost hidden in rocky depressions.

239 *Metandrocarpa taylori*

Social. Height to about 6 millimeters (¼ inch). Zooids are hemispherical, attached to surfaces by a flattened base and interconnected by branching stolons, which may disappear after a time. Red-orange.

From Prince William Sound to California. Primarily subtidal but occasionally in low intertidal zone. Found on hard surfaces. May be locally abundant.

240 ? *Clavelina* sp.

Social. Height of zooid to 1.3 centimeters (½ inch) or more. Zooids are connected by stolons from which new zooids may bud; zooids clublike and separated from each other along their whole length. Apertures on short tubes at the anterior end of zooid. Colonies may include dozens of individuals. Tunic, transparent.

Species of *Clavelina* occur from Southeastern Alaska to California. Subtidal. Found on hard surfaces.

241 ? *Trididemnum* sp.

Compound. An irregular encrusting growth, diameter to 15.2 centimeters (6 inches) or more. Colony firm, with minute, starlike, calcareous spicules. Zooids arranged in extensive, branching systems. Each zooid with its own incurrent opening, often indicated on the surface of the colony by a clear spot surrounded by a grouping of spicules. Each excurrent opening shared by many zooids (one or a few excurrent openings in a colony). Colony, gray, tinged with pink.

Species of *Trididemnum* occur from the Chukchi Sea to California. Subtidal. Occurs on rock surfaces.

Glossary

Aboral. The side opposite that on which the mouth is located (used in connection with radially symmetrical animals).

Amorphous. Without definite form.

Amphipod. A small crustacean belonging to the order Amphipoda.

Aperture. An opening; in gastropod shells, the opening out of which the soft animal extends itself.

Apex. The highest point; in gastropod shells, the peak, or point from which spiral growth began.

Aragonite. One type of crystalline calcium carbonate.

Article. In crustaceans, each unit of a jointed appendage.

Axial. Pertaining to or parallel to axis.

Basal. With reference to a base or something pertaining to a base.

Bell. In a jellyfish (medusa), the gelatinous, cup-shaped portion of the animal.

Benthic. With reference to aquatic animals and plants that live on or in substrates, rather than floating, swimming or being carried about by currents.

Bilobed. With two lobes.

Byssal. Referring to a byssus, a group of threads secreted by certain molluscs as a means of attachment.

Calcareous. Composed of calcium carbonate.

Callus. In gastropods, a thickening of the shell near or over the umbilicus.

Canal. In a gastropod shell, the tubular extension of the aperture which accommodates the animal's siphon.

Cancellate. Referring to a pattern of external sculpturing on mollusc shells; forming a network or lattice by the intersection of lines or ridges.

Capitulum. In a gooseneck barnacle, the top, plate-covered portion of the animal.

Carapace. In crustaceans, the hard covering of the cephalothorax.

Carnivore. An animal that feeds on other animals.

Carpus. In crustaceans, the fifth segment of a leg (counting from the base); on the cheliped, the segment adjacent to that which is modified into a pincer.

Carrion. Dead and decaying flesh.

Cephalothorax. In crustaceans, the body area which consists of the joined head and thorax and is covered by the carapace.

Ceras (pl. cerata). In nudibranchs, a fleshy projection on the dorsal surface which functions in respiration.

Chela (pl. chelae). In crustaceans, a pincer in which the dactyl is movable and the adjacent segment (propodus) is stationary.

Cheliped. In crustaceans, a leg which bears a pincer, or chela, at its tip.

Chitin. A semitransparent, horny material that is a principal part of crustacean exoskeletons.

Chitinous. Containing chitin.

Chromatophore. A cell that contains pigment and that by expansion or contraction contributes to color change in the skin.

Cilia. Microscopic, hairlike projections often capable of a rapid beating movement.

Ciliary. Referring to cilia.

Cirrus (pl. cirri). A filamentlike appendage; in barnacles, a featherlike appendage of the thorax used for gathering food.

Colloblast. In ctenophores, an adhesive cell used to capture food.

Columnella. In gastropods, the central pillar of a spiral shell.

Comb. Among members of the Ctenophora, transverse rows of ciliated paddles that are rhythmically raised, then flattened in order to propel the animal through the water; the combs are arranged in longitudinal rows.

Commensal. With reference to an organism that derives benefit (food or shelter) from another, different organism without harming or benefiting the latter.

Copepod. A small crustacean at times abundant in plankton.

Coralline algae. A group of red algae characterized by their hard, pink, calcareous structure; may grow in erect or encrusting forms.

Crenulation. Minute notches or scalloped projections, sometimes occurring, for example, on the inner edge of a bivalve shell.

Dactyl. In crustaceans, the terminal segment of a leg, usually pointed and clawlike.

Deposit feeder. An animal that feeds by ingesting silt or similar matter and internally separating often microscopic food from it.

Detritus. Loose particles or fragments of decaying organic material.

Diatom. Single-celled microscopic alga with wall of silica.

Dorsal. With reference to the back or upper side of an organism.

Elliptical. Having the shape of an ellipse.

Elytra. Scales that occur on and cover much of the dorsal surface of polychaetes of the Polynoidae and related families, called scale worms.

Eversible. Capable of being turned inside-out or outward.

Excurrent. With reference to an outward-flowing current.

Filter feeder. An animal that feeds by straining small organisms or detritus from the surrounding water.

Flagellum (pl. flagella). A slender extension of a cell capable of waving or whipping motion and functioning in locomotion, attachment, or creation of water currents.

Girdle. In chitons, the firm mantle which encircles the valves and in some species partly or completely covers them.

Globose. With a shape like or nearly like a sphere.

Gonad. An organ that produces either eggs or sperm.

Gonophores. In hydroid colonies, a structure which includes a reproductive structure.

Gorgonian. A member of a group of Cnidarians that are supported by an internal, horny core, and generally grow in a branching, fan-like form.

Gullet. A passageway between the mouth and the organs or area where digestion takes place.

Herbivore. An animal that feeds on plants.

Hermaphroditic. Referring to an individual organism that has both male and female reproductive organs.

Hippolytid. A shrimp belonging to the group Hippolytidae.

Hydromedusa (pl. hydromedusae). The medusoid, or jellyfish, stage among members of the group Hydrozoa.

Hydrotheca (pl. hydrothecae). In hydroids, the hard covering that surrounds an individual feeding polyp.

Incise. To cut into the surface, as an incised line.

Incurrent. With reference to an inflowing current.

Lamella (pl. lamellae). A thin layer or plate; in gastropod shells, thin, outward extending axial sculpture.

Larva (pl. larvae). The newly hatched or early stage of an animal that differs markedly in form from the adults of the species.

Lateral. With reference to the side or sides.

Longitudinal. With reference to the length; lengthwise.

Lophophore. In phoronids, bryozoans, and brachiopods, a ridged or folded structure with ciliated tentacles used in respiration and in collecting food from passing water currents.

Madreporite. In sea stars and urchins, a perforated plate near the center of the aboral surface which may permit water to enter the water-vascular system.

Mandibles. The first pair of mouth parts in Arthropods.

Mantle. In shell-bearing molluscs and brachiopods, a layer of soft tissue which secretes the shell; in nudibranchs, the tissue covering the dorsal surface of the animal; in cephalopods, the sac-like covering of the body.

Manubrium. In medusae, a stalk which hangs down from the central underside of the bell and bears the animal's mouth.

Marginal. With reference to an edge.

Median. Located in the middle; lying in a plane that divides a bilaterally symmetrical animal or structure into a left and right half.

Medusa (pl. medusae). A free-swimming jellyfish, an animal usually consisting of gelatinous bell, mouth centrally located beneath the bell, and tentacles originating on the bell.

Medusoid. With reference to a medusa, or jellyfish.

Membranous. Composed of a thin, skinlike layer of tissue.

Metamorphose. To transform, change in form or structure.

Nacreous. With reference to the innermost of the three layers of mollusc shells; often used to mean pearly, a quality sometimes possessed by a nacreous layer.

Nematocyst. In cnidarians, a capsule with an eversible internal filament that stings or lassos prey and aids in their capture.

Operculum (pl. opercula). A hard plate covering an aperture; found in many gastropods, tube worms and bryozoans.

Oral. Of the mouth, or the surface on which the mouth is located.

Osculum (pl. oscula). In a sponge, a relatively large opening through which water flows out of the body mass.

Papilla (pl. papillae). A small, fleshy projection or protuberance.

Papula (pl. papulae). In echinoderms, small, numerous, soft projections that function in respiration.

Parapodia. In polychaete worms, lateral paired projections on the segments.

Paxilla (pl. paxillae). In sea stars, a columnlike calcareous structure on the body surface that may be topped by minute tubercles or spines.

Pedicel. A stalklike structure; in brachiopods the stalk that attaches the animal to the substrate.

Pedicellaria (pl. pedicellariae). In sea stars and urchins, a minute, pincerlike structure often borne on a stalk.

Peduncle. A stalklike structure.

Periostracum. In molluscs, the outer organic covering on the shell.

Pincer. In crustaceans, the last two articles of a leg if they oppose each other.

Pinnate. Having a featherlike structure which projects from both sides of a central axis.

Plankton. Small, often microscopic, plants and animals that drift or swim weakly.

Polyp. A cnidarian with a cylindrical body and an oral opening surrounded by tentacles.

Polypoid. Pertaining to a polyp; shaped like an anemone.

Predatory. With reference to the act of preying on other living animals.

Proboscis. In worms, a slender structure that can be everted from the mouth and used in feeding.

Process. A structure that extends or projects.

Radial. Arranged like wheel spokes; radiating from a central point.

Radula (pl. radulae). In molluscs, a flexible, ribbonlike band with rows of teeth.

Rhinophores. In nudibranchs, a pair of tentacles borne on the dorsal side of the head; often elaborate with many lamellae.

Rostrum. In crustaceans, a forward-pointing projection or prolongation of the carapace located between the eyes.

Septum (pl. septa). A thin partition between two cavities or areas.

Sessile. Permanently attached, not free moving.

Seta (pl. setae). A structure that is slender and bristlelike.

Siliceous. Containing or consisting of silica.

Sinuous. Characterized by curves and turns.

Siphon. A tubular structure through which water is taken in or expelled.

Social. With reference to species in which individuals occur in clusters and reproduce asexually by stolons.

Spicule. One of the small microscopic silicate or calcium carbonate structures that make up the skeleton of certain sponges and soft corals. Also found in some ascidians.

Spongin. A fibrous material that forms the skeletal structure of some sponges.

Stolon. A long, slender, sometimes threadlike structure from which new individuals may bud.

Striate. The state of being marked by thin lines or grooves.

Striation. A thin line or groove, often occurring in multiples and forming a surface texture.

Stylet. A small, sharply pointed projection.

Substrate. The surface upon which a plant or animal grows or that to which it is attached.

Suture. A seamlike joint; in gastropod shells, the line which marks the juncture of whorls of the shell.

Symbiotic. Referring to two organisms that live in close functional association with each other; sometimes with mutual benefit to both.

Tentacle. A slender, flexible, unsegmented protrusion such as those that surround the oral disc of an anemone or fringe the bell of a jellyfish.

Test. In sea urchins, the hard, globose, internal skeleton made up of many small, calcareous plates.

Thorax. The midsection of a body between head and abdomen.

Transverse. Situated crosswise.

Tubercle. A small, rounded knob or protuberance.

Tunic. In sea squirts or other urochordates, the outer covering.

Umbilicus. In gastropod shells, a small opening at the base of the shell, leading into the central pillar around which the shell spirals as it grows.

Valve. One of the pieces forming the shell of a mollusc; a clam has two valves, and a chiton eight valves.

Variant. That which may belong to a certain group yet differs from the group in some of its characteristics.

Varix (pl. varices). In gastropod shells, a prominent ridge across the whorl, which indicates a former lip, or edge of the aperture.

Velum (pl. vela). A membrane that extends inward like a shelf from the margin of a jellyfish. Characteristic of hydromedusae.

Ventral. With reference to the lower surface of an animal.

Visceral. Referring to internal organs, particularly those involved in digestion.

Whorl. In gastropods, a complete spiral turn of the shell.

Zoanthid. An anemone that grows in colonies with the bases of the polyps in the group connected.

Zooecium (pl. zooecia). In bryozoans, the calcareous or chitinous structure that encases an individual zooid.

Zooid. One of the often microscopic animals that make up a colony; used in reference to such groups as bryozoans and hydroids.

Zooplankton. Small, often microscopic animals in water.

Selected Bibliography

In preparing the manuscript for this book, we have gathered information from a great many printed sources. Many materials used were from scientific journals or technical publications available only in specialized libraries. The list which follows is not comprehensive but does include references we have used that may be readily accessible to the general reader.

Abbott, R.T. 1974. *American seashells.* 2d ed. New York: Van Nostrand Reinhold.

Behrens, D.W. 1980. *Pacific coast nudibranchs. A guide to the opisthobranchs of the northeastern pacific.* Los Osos, California: Sea Challengers.

Cornwall, I.E. 1969. *The barnacles of British Columbia.* 2d ed. Handbook No. 7. British Columbia Provincial Museum.

Griffith, L.M. 1975. *The intertidal univalves of British Columbia.* Handbook No. 26. Victoria: British Columbia Provincial Museum.

Johnson, M.E. and H.J. Snook. 1967. *Seashore animals of the pacific coast.* Dover ed. New York: Dover Publications.

Keen, A.M. and E. Coan. 1974. *Marine molluscan genera of western north america. An Illustrated Key.* 2d ed. Stanford: Stanford University Press.

Kozloff, E.N. 1973. *Seashore life of Puget Sound, the Strait of Georgia, and the San Juan Archipelago.* Seattle: University of Washington Press.

———. 1974. *Keys to the marine invertebrates of Puget Sound, the San Juan Archipelago, and adjacent regions.* Seattle: University of Washington Press.

MacGinitie, G.E. and N. MacGinitie. 1968. *Natural history of marine animals.* 2d ed. New York: McGraw-Hill.

Meglitsch, P.A. 1972. *Invertebrate zoology.* 2d ed. New York: Oxford University Press.

Morris, P.A. 1966. *A field guide to pacific coast shells.* 2d ed. Peterson Field Guide Series. Boston: Houghton Mifflin.

Quayle, D.B. 1970. *The intertidal bivalves of British Columbia.* Handbook No. 17. Victoria: British Columbia Provincial Museum.

Ricketts, E.F. and J. Calvin. Revised by J.W. Hedgpeth. 1968. *Between pacific tides.* 4th ed. Stanford: Stanford University Press.

Smith, R.I. and J.T. Carlton, eds. 1975. *Light's manual. Intertidal invertebrates of the central California coast.* 3d ed. Berkeley: University of California Press.

Index

An italicized number is for the page of a species' photograph. A number shown in bold refers to the species' primary textual discussion.